I0169897

The One Year Marriage

A Formula for Enduring Love

Revised Edition

G. S. Renfrey, Ph.D.

MOONTIDE

Published by Moontide Books
49 Seymour Crescent
Barrie, Ontario
L4N 8N4

www.moontidebooks.com
moontidebooks@gmail.com

ঌ•ৡ

Copyright © G. S. Renfrey, 2018
{Original Edition Copyrighted in 2013}

All rights reserved. No part of this book may be
reproduced in any form, by any means, electronic or
mechanical, including information storage and retrieval
systems, without the publisher's written permission.

This is an original work, conceived and developed
entirely by the author. Citations have been given where
appropriate. Any similarities to un-cited material that is
not a part of the general fund of public knowledge is
merely coincidental.

ঌ•ৡ

Edited by Elizabeth Eilert Grewal
Editorial & content contributions by Dee Chinimini
Cover Artwork by Darkmoon 1968

Canadian Cataloguing in Publications data

ISBN 978-0-9921699-0-9

Printed in the USA

Acknowledgements

I am deeply grateful to everyone who has contributed to this book. To my clients who, over the past 28 years, have taught me so much about what does and does not work in relationships, my many thanks and best wishes. To the readers of the first edition who shared their thoughts, feelings, and experiences with the One Year marriage model, thank you so much – you've been instrumental to this revised edition.

To the friends and colleagues with whom I've discussed the concept and content of this book for some years now, thank you for your insight and frank feedback.

To Ms. Dee Chinimini, thank you for your support and encouragement, your often-challenging feedback, and for contributing a feminine perspective to the book through your sage advice.

To Elizabeth Eilert Grewal, thank you for bringing your mastery of the written language to this revised version.

The Poem

A Moment

We only have a moment with one another
A moment to glance, to laugh
to dance a dance with each other …
and then it ends
Although at times it feels like forever
it really is only a moment
So laugh your hardest, smile your brightest
cry every tear you have
Love your fullest for a moment is all we have
No regrets, no "what ifs"
No forgotten words still needing to be said
For all we have is one moment
to pass our smile, our imprint on
and then the dance must end

Dinaz. August, 2002

Contents

Preface To The Revised Version

"The significant problems we face cannot be solved at the same level of thinking we were at when we created them." ~ **Albert Einstein**

As I prepared to write the preface for this revised version of The One Year Marriage, my thoughts took me back to that day on a beach in California when the concept crystallized for me. It was an alchemical moment when years of study, contemplation, and clinical experience came together in a flash of insight. As in traditional alchemy, the process produced what I believe to be something as precious as gold: a simple formula that could help couples come together in loving unions in a way that would endure and promote their individual and collective growth.

In the years since its first publication in 2013 I have become even more convinced, through further study, clinical application, and feedback of the viability and benefits of the One Year Marriage Model. I also believe that it is even more relevant to relationships now than it was five years ago and will likely become even more so in the coming years.

Below I have provided a lightly doctored version of the original preface. I've included it because it makes important points to consider when reading the book. Before that, however, I want to make a few comments about this revised version.

My original intention with the revised version was to populate it with considerably more references, an inclination I have given my background in basic and applied research. Despite having collected well over 100 citable references since the initial publication in 2013, however, I have decided to forgo that approach. This book is not intended to be a research paper nor does it set out to prove any particular point. What the book is intended to be are thought provoking and an aid for readers to examine their own ideals and beliefs about relationships so that they can make more informed and conscious choices. I have included new references where I thought readers might want to explore an issue or a point a little further but I've tried to avoid overdoing this.

Another point I want to make which may prove critical to you getting the most of this book is to read what follows with an open mind. I am not asking you the reader to accept the position I've taken on relationships nor am I attempting to change your thoughts or hopes about marriage. However, because the proposed remodelling of marriage and relationships strikes most people as being radical if not downright shocking, it is important that you not close yourself off from giving the ideas presented your fair consideration.

Although I make this point later on in the book, I want to 'pre-peat' it here: the One Year Marriage model can be used in a formal manner as described herein, but most readers will not, even if so inclined. Instead, they will opt to use it in whole or in part to inform choices they make in whatever relationship model they use. Whether a couple is living together, engaging and a premarital dry run, or is formally married in the Western tradition, applying even some of the principles presented here can improve the quality and longevity of their relationship, and their collective and personal happiness. Because of this I do hope you will read with an open heart and an open mind.

…GS Renfrey, January 31, 2018

Imagine your ideal romantic relationship. What does that look like? What does it feel like? Most of us hold some notion of an idyllic romantic bond in our minds, a heartfelt sense of how things could or should be when we find that special person with whom to share our lives. Sadly, for majority of us the reality of romantic unions is not idyllic, and falls short of what we yearn for. Why is that? Are our dreams and expectations unrealistic? Have we just not found the right person yet? Are we, or our partners, doing something wrong? Is it actually possible to have a relationship that can fulfill our deepest desires?

I puzzled with those questions for years in the course of my clinical work, and in watching friends dance into relationships only to crawl out of them a few years later. I also experienced first hand my own bittersweet pangs of love found and lost. The clinical writings on the matter and the myriad of self-help books on relationships often point out core factors deemed important to a successful marriage. These include: the ability to form effective attachments to others; having congruent worldviews and life-goals; having congruent approaches to parenting and finances; and having good, respectful communication to name a few.

I also pondered what many spiritual and philosophical traditions had to say on the matter as well, each embodying their own wisdom and directives for a long and happy union. Nothing I encountered impressed me as being a viable prescription, in and of itself, for a long and happy relationship. None of the wisdom from the behavioural sciences, philosophies, or spiritual traditions was broad enough, deep enough, or specific and practical enough. What was missing for me was a simple yet comprehensive model of how romantic relationships should be done – a prescription for enduring love.

I believe this book offers just such a prescription, though it is one you and your beloved will have to co-write. How did I discover it? Well, have you ever struggled with a puzzle or problem that, despite your best efforts, seemed to defy solution? Have you ever then had the experience of suddenly seeing the challenge from a completely new perspective and have the solution unfold itself before your eyes? Often what sets the stage for such an "ah ha" experience is stepping away from the problem for a while and coming back to it with a clear mind space.

Life is filled with examples of this simple truth: when faced with a puzzle that resists resolution, the best answers often arise after we relax our assumptions about what the real problem is and how we ought to go about solving it. Einstein's Special Theory of Relativity is one result of such unconfined thinking. A great example of confined thinking is seen in the words of Charles Duell who, in 1899 as the director of the U.S. Patent office declared, "Everything that can be invented, has been invented."

Birth of an Idea

I had my epiphany while walking with a friend of mine along an otherwise deserted California beach. My friend was going through a difficult separation with his partner of eight years and everything that he spoke about I had heard countless times before during marital and divorce counselling. Love and commitment had faded over the years, worn away by hurt and disappointment. What remained were anger, disillusionment, and fear.

I quickly thought about the couples I knew or had known through my adult years and concluded that I'd met only a handful that seemed truly happy with themselves and each other. What's more, the majority of partnered people I've known seemed to have compromised something important to their souls, their life journeys, for the sake of their marriages. Some were aware of this but many were not. More disturbing, many couples I'd worked with knew they were terribly unhappy with their marriages but felt trapped in them – trapped because of fear of starting over or of being alone, the shame of failure, financial enmeshment, or concerns for the welfare of their children. Words from an old tune drifted into my mind and seemed to capture the state of far too many marriages: "…hanging on in quiet desperation…" [Pink Floyd – *Time*]. I intuitively knew there had to be a way to prevent all the pain and madness suffered in the name of marriage.

As we trekked along that serene beach, deep into reflective discussion, thematic threads began to emerge and weave an idea in my mind. Then it came into razor-sharp focus: what if couples approached a relationship / marriage as though it were a one-year renewable contract? I offered it up to the discussion and after a few moments of silence, potential problems with the concept became our focus, not the least of which was public acceptance. The more we discussed it, however, the more sense it made to me. The One Year Marriage (OYM) was born.

In the months that followed, I explored the concept from every angle through deep contemplations, theoretical analyses, discussions, and careful mini-experiments with my clients. After two years of that, I was convinced that the idea was not a half-baked or naïve notion that had no place in the real world, but possibly a viable new paradigm for marriage.

If this idea has already horrified you, let me clarify something very important: I do believe it is possible to find a great love and cultivate a relationship that will bring profound and lasting satisfaction. I firmly believe it is within the grasp of each of us to co-create the sort of relationship that, at its heart, captures the essence of what most of us long for. I also believe, however, that to realize this sort of love we need to alter some of our assumptions about relationships, and change our very way of doing them.

Imagine the following: You are in a relationship with someone you like, love, and respect. You know, without a doubt, that your partner also loves, likes, and respects you. You never feel constrained by your partner's expectations or insecurities, but feel supported in pursuing your dreams regardless of the direction they may take you. You also feel secure in supporting your partner's dreams and life path. The two of you conduct the busyness of your lives like happy partners in a well-run business, and always spend enough quality time together, enjoying each other in the love you share.

You and your partner have the willingness and capacity to endure hard times together. The two of you can meet the inevitable challenges that life and relationships bring, and can succeed with confidence and courage. You are in the relationship only because you truly want to be, as is your partner, since you both know that dissolving it would carry no burden other than healthy grieving. Nothing binds the two of you together except your love for each other and your desire to remain together. Each of you is like a sovereign ruler of your own realm, sharing your life, your love, and the resources of your realms, only until such a time as you would do otherwise.

How does that sound to you? If you're like most people, you may react with a mixture of likes, dislikes, and reservations – perfectly normal and expected. I hope, however, that by the time you finish this book you will have explored your dislikes and reservations. Perhaps you may even come to accept a few new ideas about what a healthy relationship looks like and how to create one. You have nothing to lose except some old ideas that may be preventing you from realizing the dream of a great love.

My Intention with This Book

As I stated in the fist edition, my intention with this book is not to further erode the institution of marriage as some might fear when they hear of the concept. Marriage, as the Western world has traditionally viewed it, has already been eroded to the point where a large and growing number no longer consider it a viable institution. I don't want to inflict even more damage. A OYM is still two people coming together to share their lives in love and happiness. What I propose is simply a new way of doing it that I believe will be more effective in helping people get what they deeply want from marriage and ensuring that it endures. In the event that the union does not endure, the OYM is designed to make dissolution fair and as pain free as possible.

I believe in marriage as a commitment of love. I believe it can be a means for two people to come together in a way that makes their individual lives larger and more meaningful. At heart, I'm a romantic – I believe love can be for a lifetime, that it can conquer most anything, and I like to think we can each find a soul mate or two in this lifetime. I also believe all people, regardless of this gender identification, can and must be genuine to themselves and their essential natures within marriage. I believe that all genders can benefit equally from the union.

With so much potential for happiness available to each of us, I'm saddened by the unhappiness I encounter among married couples, both professionally and personally. My motivation for writing this book was to offer a possible antidote for this. The cure comes in the form of a new way of doing relationships; a new model for marriage that will not only help people cultivate happier and more enduring unions, but perhaps more effective, satisfying lives as well.

In this edition, my intention remains the same – offer an

alternative to the traditional model of marriage that continues to decline in both success and popularity. It is also to provide individuals and couples with a means to explore their hopes and expectations regarding relationships; I believe these are, in fact, frequent reasons that marriages erode from the joyous unions they start out as.

How to Get the Most from This Book

To benefit most from this book, I recommend that you read it with an open mind and a serving of emotional and intellectual courage. A simple curiosity about how you might be able to use the concept and the exercises to improve your relationships can set a good tone. Remember, you don't have to accept anything without question or everything as a whole. As is often suggested within many traditions of wisdom, take what you find helpful and leave the rest.

For the reader who resists the notion of changing up marriage, I want to point out that marriage has already changed over time, only not as rapidly as Western society has; in many ways, it's been left behind. What I am proposing is not as radical as it might first seem – it's simply a new way to approach this most important of relationships to bring it up to speed with our modern ethos and realities.

Some statements in the book are generalizations that may or may not apply to a given reader. Some statements may even seem sexist or old school, particularly when it comes to addressing gender differences, but I assure you they are not. Nevertheless, I anticipate that most readers will have at least some objections to what they will read. When this happens, it likely means something good is in process – your ideas about marriage and relationships are being challenged in some way and that means it is an opportunity to examine those ideas and either reaffirm or alter them. In either case, that is a benefit to you.

What we accept or object to can teach us a lot about ourselves. When we find a concept or idea pleasing, it usually means that it's helpful to our understanding or that it resonates well with held beliefs. Conversely, when we find an idea upsetting, it often means that it doesn't fit our current model of how the world works, or transgresses a value or belief we hold. The stronger the value or belief, and the more congruent or incongruent the idea is with it, the greater the reaction.

Rejecting a new idea can be a healthy reaction when it's in conflict with the way we consciously wish to conduct our lives. At the same time it can be an opportunity to explore whether held values or beliefs are still viable or outmoded. Lifelong learners and others committed to personal growth know that holding too tightly to attitudes, beliefs, or values can slow our development and prevent desired change. How do you know whether an objection is viable or archaic? Challenge it. Wisdom, after all, is the product of never taking one's opinions or ideas too seriously – they are just our best guesses about life, are always wrong to some degree, and require constant evaluation and revision.

One way to do this is to ask yourself to justify the objection and explore what you come up with. If you can make a well thought out argument for it, one that isn't based solely on negative emotions, and that argument resonates truth for you, then adhering to it may be a good choice.

Another way to challenge an objection to an idea is to temporarily set your opposition aside and ask yourself, 'in what way is this true of or for me?' An idea doesn't have to be 100% applicable to be useful, and sometimes finding even a small way that a new concept can apply to you can open doors to growth and positive change.

If you take the above approach, you will benefit from this book whether you decide to adopt the OYM model or not.

The real payoff is in how you think about your relationships and how you decide to conduct yourself within them. That will help in all of your other relationships as well, be they with friends or coworkers. In addition, the reactions that you and your companions have to the ideas in this book can speak volumes about your hopes, values, and your ideas about relationships.

Exploring these reactions and talking about them can be a fun diversion, but it can also lead to valuable insights. Exploring your emotional and intellectual reactions with a prospective partner might open both your eyes to what you are each bringing to the relationship table.

Make no mistake, a One Year Marriage is a viable option for a marital union. You could choose to follow the model closely and actually create and sign a formal agreement with your partner, or you can create an agreement of intentions. If you are already in a traditional marriage, you can still choose to "upgrade" your relationship by living together as though by a one-year agreement and still enjoy most of the benefits.

I believe that creating a formal or informal agreement with a partner while you are still in the serious dating phase (i.e., you're dating exclusively and both of you are thinking long term) can be a real benefit, even if you do not intend to follow the model when you are married. Why? Because it will give both of you a solid reality check on how much each is willing and able to follow through on stated intentions. If your prospective marriage partner cannot deliver on a negotiated, agreed on way to honour each other while dating, I can guarantee he or she won't be able to when married.

A quick note regarding terminology: most everything I have written about marriage also applies to people living together and much of it can apply to dating couples. For that reason, I tend to use the term marriage loosely and often use the term 'union' instead. Whether you are legally married, living with your partner, dating, or single, it might be useful while reading this book to think about marriage in two ways – as a legal contract between two people, and as an emotional bond, for a I will suggest shortly, it is both.

Regarding sexual categories in these gender fluid times, some readers may resist the notion of being classified as male or female. If that applies to you, not to worry – however you define yourself, the ideas put forth are relevant to you. The principles and practices of a OYM are applicable to any sort of romantic union between any number of people of any gender description. For simplicity sake, however, I have tended to reference the masculine and feminine.

Regarding cultural bias, this book is written for a Western readership. Although there are usually greater differences between people within cultures as there are between cultures, this book does have a Western bias. Cultures provide the social context within which we live and as such they provide many if not most of our frames and reference and beliefs. The impact that cultural indoctrinations have on our perceptions of self and the world around us cannot be underestimated. Sometimes concepts and beliefs from one culture, as functional and beneficial as they might be, do not fit well within another. However, readers from other cultural backgrounds or Western subcultures can still gain insight into their attitudes and beliefs about marriage and relationships through this book.

I've included case examples to help illustrate certain points. All such examples are based, in whole or in part, on real cases. The names and other potentially identifying information have been changed, however, to preserve the confidentiality and privacy of the people involved.

Regarding cited resources, these were intended to be indicative and suggestive, not exhaustive. A review of the literature prior to this revised edition did not uncover newer material that would justifiably replace the references previously used, though some have been added.

Finally, those who shared their feedback and stories after reading the first edition of the OYM have played a valuable role in the evolution of this revised edition. I invite you to share your comments about this book, relationships, or any of your own relationship explorations by email directed to oneyearmarriage@gmail.com.

Let us begin...

Chapter 1

Love and Marriage Under Siege

"Love, the strongest and deepest element in all life, the harbinger of hope, of joy, of ecstasy; love, the defier of all laws, of all conventions; love, the freest, the most powerful molder of human destiny; how can such an all-compelling force be synonymous with that poor little State- and Church-begotten weed, marriage?" ~ **Emma Goldman**

Marriage: An Outdated Concept?

There is no denying it – marriage, as we know it, is under siege. Traditional marriage is declining in both success and popularity, yet we continue to uphold it as the standard for people in love to join their lives by. Many of us hold high hopes and expectations for marriage and yet, as an institution, it hasn't had a serious review and revision for centuries. That suggests two important things to me: (1) what people hope marriage will do for them remains important; and (2) how we think about and do marriage may be overdue for an upgrade. Though marriage does appear to be an institution in decline, I believe life still stirs amid the ashes of the marital pyre, and that change may enable it to rise like the proverbial phoenix.

In this chapter, I'll briefly explore what people are most often looking for in marriage, which I'll do in much greater detail in chapters three and four, and then discuss what I believe are the main reasons why marriage so often fails to deliver what we hope. You don't have to share my perceptions or accept my prepositions to get a lot from this chapter. You will benefit nevertheless by contemplating and

19

identifying the reasons you believe relationships fail.

Let's begin first by clarifying the use of the term marriage. For our purposes, I've chosen the definition in Wikipedia (See http://en.wikipedia.org/wiki/Marriage) as it seems less heterosexist and cultural-centric than many.

> *Marriage (or wedlock) is a social union or legal contract between people that creates kinship. It is an institution in which interpersonal relationships, usually intimate and sexual, are acknowledged in a variety of ways, depending on the culture or subculture in which it is found. Such a union, often formalized via a wedding ceremony, may also be called matrimony.*

In this book, I've used the terms marriage, union, and relationship synonymously, in accordance with this broad definition. By contrast, I have used the term "traditional marriage" to mean the institution as most commonly understood and practiced in the Western world.

What Do People Want From Marriage?

Answers to this question will vary from person to person and, as we shall explore in chapters three and four, can differ between genders. Though the only answers to this question that count are your own, there are some common desires that hold true for many.

One of those desires is the simple wish for a companion to make doing life easier and more enjoyable compared to doing it all alone. Another is the sense of security and comfort a committed, healthy relationship can bring. Let's face it; in this increasingly cold and disconnected world, knowing there is a warm body and familiar smile when we get home has a certain appeal. Add to that the belief that this special and trusted person will be there for us when we need them, and you foster a sense of belonging and security, both of which are deep, fundamental needs.

Then there is sex, wonderful sex – the glue that holds romantic relationships together. Having a reliable and enthusiastic partner for lovemaking can be one of life's great joys. In a culture still haunted by taboos against sex and plagued by the reality of STDs, having someone special to safely share the gift of sex and lovemaking is a big draw.

With sex, children have a way of appearing. Procreation is a powerful life drive; from a biological point of view, it ranks about fourth after breathing, drinking, and eating. All that sexual desire and joy is nature's way of ensuring we make babies, though humans and bonobo chimps have expanded the role of sex into that of a social adhesive and recreational activity. Whether planned or gifted, the arrival of children means years of dedication, sacrifice, and hard work for most. Does anyone want to do that alone?

"What about love," as the saying goes? Now we're getting to the heart of the matter – love and partnership are the emotional core of what most people want from marriage. Most of us long for a deep, abiding love that will endure the tests of time and tribulation. Although few appear to achieve that, the desire lives on.

We want a great love, a partner with whom to share our lives. Even after the heart-racing craziness of love's infatuation phase diminishes, so much more awaits us in a committed relationship. When we accomplish something we're proud of, we want someone to share that with, who will get as much joy out of it as we do. When we fail at something or mess up and feel lousy, we want someone special to console us and remind us that life remains sweet and that all the turmoil in the world cannot change that.

Perhaps the most satisfying part of a loving, committed relationship is the knowledge that we have someone in our lives that sees us for who we really are and still likes us. Perhaps the most important part of a long-term partnership is that we have someone to witness our lives. Each of us is a precious centre of a unique universe. Though many of us strive to find meaning in this life through deeds and accomplishments, I believe the most meaningful thing at the end of our days is that there was someone we knew and loved, who witnessed the miracle of our unique life. Traditionally, marriage has been the primary vessel for this. That institution, however, is in jeopardy today.

Marriage in Decline

As I stated in the opening sentence of the chapter, marriage as we know it is in decline. In the next few paragraphs I provide a few statistics to support this point; however, I don't intend to spend much time or page space on the numbers as they can be very deceiving. As a rule, it's a good practice to be cautious of statistics and poll results, as they are prone to misinterpretation, misrepresentation, and intentional skewing (e.g., designing a poll that will generate the results you want regardless of true public sentiment). The numbers I share with you should be taken as suggestive only. That said, I accept the common estimate that 50+% of marriages today will end in divorce as being reasonably accurate.

The numbers are a little more complicated than that – divorce rates differ depending on the age of the individuals when married (the younger the age the higher the rate), whether there are children involved (children lower the rate slightly), and whether it is the first, second, or third marriage (the rate climbs significantly with each marriage). If these stats aren't dreary enough, have you ever wondered how many couples of the slightly less than 50% who do stay together are actually happy in their marriages? By this I mean not just complacently satisfied, but truly happy. By analogy, I'm talking about the difference between having a job that you're content with, and one that you can't wait to get to work for each day. By that benchmark, I'd guess that less than 20% of marriages of more than four years are truly happy.

Perhaps more telling for me about the decline in marriage are the shifting attitudes toward it. A recent TIME/Pew research poll found that from 27% to 62% (with a 39% average) of Americans believed marriage was becoming obsolete.[1] Another study in the UK found that between 27% and 38% of women ages 18 and older (the younger the greater the percentage) thought marriage was no longer relevant.[2] Similar numbers can be found for Canada and Australia as well. Even Statistics Canada, the government agency mandated to monitor important information about Canadians to help guide government policy, has decided to stop monitoring marriage and divorce rates – it's just too low a priority and all too likely deemed irrelevant to policy making. If you research the success rates for cohabiting couples, you'll find the stats no better. At the same time, numerous polls suggest that people still hold the ideals of a marital-type union in the highest regard.

Another report that hit cyberspace while I was writing this book declared that the seven-year-itch has now contracted to three years.[3] According to the researchers, a full 67% of surveyed couples found themselves growing dissatisfied with their partners only three years into their relationship. Further, the three-year point seemed to mark a decline in the frequency of sexual activity and a decline in exchanged compliments. At the three-year mark, about one

1. www.time.com/time/interactive/0,31813,2031965,00.html
2. www.martinfrost.ws/htmlfiles/oct2006/marriage2.html#1_134_women_aged_18_surveyed
3. www.reuters.com/article/2011/03/08/us-couples-survey-idUSTRE7276UF20110308

third were pursuing activities and vacations outside of the relationship as a means of recapturing what they felt they'd lost. This didn't surprise me. Although it is disappointing that the lustre of married life seems to decline so fast so often, I believe the reaction to this of engaging in outside interests and taking separate vacations may actually be a healthy trend, something I will address in the next chapter.

These statistics and reports strongly suggest that marriages are not living up to our hopes and expectations, and for the growing number who plan to opt out of one, their expectations appear to be negative. Are those expectations wrong; do we expect too much from marriage? Alternately, is the way we think about and do marriage outdated? Does traditional marriage fail to help us realize our hopes and dreams? I believe the answer to each is yes.

Why Marriage is in Decline

Much has been written about why marriage is in decline in the Western world, and many reasons have been cited, including general moral decline, the degradation of marriage into a commodity, and changing economic and social realities for both men and women. Most of the proposed reasons that are based on research and rational analyses likely have merit; however, instead of reviewing those, I've elected to discuss those factors I believe to be essential and most relevant to this book.

For our purposes, I've defined marital failure as occurring when at least one partner no longer wants to remain in the union. I'm not referring to a transient dissatisfaction that could be worked through; I'm referring to a deep state of dissatisfaction that cannot be fixed without compromising one's core values or integrity.

So why is the popularity and success of marriage in such

decline? I believe five factors have had a profound impact: changing economic realities, a presumption of permanence, unhealthy expectations, becoming swallowed up by an under-recognized side of marriage, and a reality-fantasy gap.

1) Changing Economic Realities

Let's face it – times have changed. Women were once compelled to rely on men for their support and men were legally bound to do so once married. Sexual mores discouraged sex outside of marriage, though we all know it happened quite a bit anyway, and parenthood outside of a marital union was frowned upon for women and almost never heard of among men. All that has changed.

Women can now create their own resources in society and live quite well without the economic support of men. Men are better today at self-care and can manage their home life and health quite well without the help of women. Men and women can enjoy emotional intimacy with others and the pleasures of sexual union outside of a committed relationship. Both genders can even take pleasure in parenthood without a marital partner, though admittedly this is still easier for women than men at present.

In short, most of the 'needs' that once compelled men and women to find and keep a marriage partner have diminished or disappeared – all but one: the desire to find a great love, a soul mate, a companion with whom to share and witness each others lives. The same Times/Pew poll cited above found that 93% of respondents asserted love as a principle reason for getting married.

I don't believe this new reality has weakened marriage, quite the contrary, I believe it has liberated men and women from feeling compelled to enter into a union for reasons other than love, or to remain in one when love has ended, and has helped set the stage for marital evolution.

2) The Presumption of Permanence

The 'love is forever' fantasy is still pervasive in the psyche of most of us. As much as the stats and our personal experiences might suggest otherwise, we seem to hold onto that notion with a firm grasp – it's how it should be – and we hope that our love will beat the odds and endure. Further, it strikes many that admitting to love's possible impermanence and contemplating such when entering a marriage (e.g., through a prenuptial agreement), is somehow unromantic or indicates a lack of faith in the relationship. I believe just the opposite to be true.

> *I have come to believe that the presumption of permanence, of enduring love, is one of the mistakes that couples make that sets the stage for marital failure.*

That is not to say that love cannot endure; it is the **presumption** of perpetuity, the belief that marriage is secure by its very nature that causes difficulties.

Throughout this book, I will sometimes make generalizations that may or may not apply to a given reader. In identifying some of the ways men and women tend to differ in response to traditional marriage, those generalizations may even appear sexist or old school. As suggested in the preface, however, setting aside your objections and reading with an open mind, asking yourself how is this or might this be true of you, will help you get the most from this exploration.

So how does the presumption of permanence set the stage for marital failure? One of the principle ways is through the perception that there will always be time to resolve issues and take care of problems that arise in the relationship. After all, doesn't it make sense that if you're gong to spend the next 60 or 70 years together, the two of you will eventually work out all the problems you encounter? That can be a costly assumption if it enables couples to let issues slide, as opposed to dealing with them immediately and effectively.

Another ill effect of the assumption of permanence is that it encourages people to lose themselves in their marriage. By this, I mean they are more likely to set aside or seriously alter their personal dreams, goals, and/or careers for the good of the marriage. On a deeper level, by assuming your sovereign "I" is now and forever a sacred "we," people can slowly lose their sense of self. This inevitably means sacrificing what you need to do to ensure your continued growth as a person, in the name of the greater good of the marriage. It can mean giving up habits, hobbies, and friends that are important to you, and supplanting them with those deemed important to the marriage. Though it is less true these days, this has been a more common problem for women than men, especially when children become part of the scene.

I've encountered far too many women in their late thirties and forties who find themselves in an existential crisis once their children have left or are about to leave for college. They find themselves uncertain of what to do with their lives, or in extreme cases, uncertain of who they are when not defined by their family responsibilities. This is surprisingly true of many career women as well, since women still tend to be the primary caregivers in dual career families.

A related way that both men and women can compromise themselves is by becoming swallowed up by their work or careers. This involves working too hard or staying in a job or career that no longer interests them solely because it has become a critical means to support the family. This is a tricky one to critique because maintaining a source of income, whether single or married, is an economic necessity for most. However, when one's personal identity and autonomy becomes compromised, trudging on in meaningless, joyless work, can result in a loss of self so profound as to result in one of the poet T.S. Eliot's "*Hollow Men*." Men have historically fallen prey to this more often than women.

Another problem with the assumption of permanence is that it tends to cultivate the assumption that one's partner will be there tomorrow, the next day, and so on. Though a sense of continuity and stability is needed in a strong, secure relationship, the assumption of permanence sets the stage for complacency and taking one's partner for granted. What is it, after all, to take something or someone for granted?

> **If you think about it, isn't assuming marital permanence the same as assuming one's partner will simply be there, and is that not synonymous with taking someone 'as granted'?**

At the risk of sounding sexist, my experience suggests that men edge out women on making this mistake, and once children come along, taking the permanence of the relationship as 'granted' becomes even more entrenched. It seems that many knowingly or unknowingly assume that children will bind a couple tighter together, make the prospect of one's partner leaving you less likely either because of the connection with the children or because of the economic complications of divorcing when children are involved.

Another reason why the belief in marital permanence is destructive is that it encourages long-range fantasies about one's partner and the relationship. It's natural to think about our partners and relationships, but quite often our thinking is a projection of our own perceptions, hopes, and fears. If we do it too much, too often, and we don't ground ourselves sufficiently in the realities of the union, we can end up living more of a virtual relationship (in our heads) with a partner of our own creation. I believe the presumption of marital permanence encourages this to the degree that many couples end up living a fantasy marriage, a myth of their own making.

The relationship fantasies we all carry around usually begin the moment we lay eyes on someone we are attracted to, or at least start during the first date. The moment we create fantasies about the person, what s/he is up to now, what it would be like to be with them, etc., we begin to craft a virtual partner. As long as we minimize this and are good at realigning the internal image with the real deal by way of reality checks, then little harm is done. All too often, however, people spend as much time talking to the imagined partner in their head as to the real one. An entire "life" can evolve in our minds, consisting of imagined interactions.

Anything that encourages us to create fantasies about our partners will tend to worsen this problem. In that vein, what could be more risky than imagining growing old with one's partner? That may be something the two of you will enjoy some day, but to fantasize about it is to create a virtual future, one that isn't real. The primary danger here is the inevitable rise of expectations.

3) Destructive Expectations

A third major reason for marital deterioration is found in the unhealthy expectations that arise between lovers.

> *Unhealthy expectations are a major cause of marital distress and demise.*

First let's clarify the difference between healthy and unhealthy expectations. Put simply, healthy expectations are those that arise from conscious mutual agreements while unhealthy ones arise unilaterally.

For example, if I tell you I'll meet you for lunch at noon, then you can reasonably expect me to show up at noon or let you know otherwise. These sorts of expectations are both contractual and transparent. Without them, it would be impossible to conduct day-to-day business with each other.

If, however, when we do meet for lunch I have an expectation that you will pay, simply because you have in the past or because you make more money than I do, that could prove to be an unhealthy and destructive expectation. What makes it unhealthy is that it stems from an assumption of mine that you may not share. It would be tantamount to me demanding that you share my assumptions and behave in accordance with them. Such non-negotiated, unilateral expectations are corrosive.

Sadly, most relationships overflow with unilateral expectations, each with the capacity to diminish the bond between two people, some with the capacity to blow it apart.

Example: John and Maggie have been married for five years. John often spoke to Maggie during their courtship about his love of children and desire to have one or two. Maggie said little to nothing on the matter and John assumed that she was on board with the plan to have kids. Five years into the marriage, however, when John began to suggest it might be time to become parents, Maggie informed him that she did not want children and never did. John and Maggie found themselves on the road to divorce.

Many toxic expectations are deeply embedded in our way of being, often from observations of parents during childhood, or from social conditioning. Most, however, emerge within a relationship. When couples don't clearly articulate their desires and boundaries and don't take time to formally agree on critical issues, assumptions and expectations grow in the vacuum of communication. If couples had a way of articulating these and formally discussing them, this sort of trouble could be prevented.

Similar and related to non-negotiated expectations, numerous unspoken agreements usually form between couples, often beginning at the first date. These are the unacknowledged and often unconscious adjustments couples make to fit into each other's lives. Although unspoken agreements that are consciously made can be quite healthy and useful, their unconscious cousins are too often compromises that we make for the sake of the relationship. These can quickly accrue to toxic levels, especially when one partner is more flexible and yielding than the other.

> *Example:* Ann noticed it on their second date – Frank had taken a quick shower before dinner at her place after they returned from a long run together. When she entered the bathroom, two towels lay on the floor and the lid to the shampoo was sitting in the drain. She didn't make anything of it; she even thought it cute as she cleaned up after him. She had no idea that by doing so and not saying anything, she was setting a bad standard that could haunt her for months to come.

Ann is trying to be flexible and easy to get along with. Instead, she is actually conveying to Frank that it is perfectly fine for him to use her shower without the courtesy cleaning up after himself. This was Ann's first step in co-creating an unspoken agreement with Frank that she would never consciously make. The flip-side is that if this happened a second and third time, Frank would form an expectation that he could impose himself on Ann in this way and perhaps in other ways as well.

As with the issue of expectations, the failure of most couples to take time to clearly articulate what does and does not work for them and then reach clear agreements often leads to unspoken agreements by default. The accumulation of these hidden expectations can slowly and surely strangle a relationship. Something then is needed to remind couples to remain conscious of how they impact each other, to achieve consensus about what does and does not work for them and to do so on a regular basis. Please make a note of that point.

An expectation that is almost guaranteed to be a lethal elixir for a marriage is that the union will fulfill you. Our deepest sense of fulfillment comes from personal growth and witnessing our lives unfold and integrate with the world around us. Having a personal purpose in life that is aligned with our deepest values and beliefs is critical to this, as is being on track with that purpose. Whether that mission is as grand as world peace or as simple as living a conscious life, as long as you remain focused on that and are in step with it, your life can be as fulfilling as humanly possible. Lacking such purpose, or being off track, we tend to feel dissatisfied and our lives can lack enthusiasm and deeper meaning.

Unfortunately, many people today are not well grounded with such purpose. As such we have a tendency to look outside ourselves for something or someone who will fill the void. That is the core motivation of all addictions and the genesis of perhaps the deadliest mistake in relationships – expecting our relationship / partner to fulfill us or make us happy.

During the infatuation phase of a new relationship, the excitement of it all can ease feelings of emptiness. However, once the novelty factor wears thin, often after only a month or year, we can become dissatisfied, even resentful and like junkies seeking another fix – we seek something new, something or someone who will, once and for all, fulfill us. So continues the cycle.

This issue of looking for something to fulfill us is a profound one and would require more time and space to cover adequately than I care to spend. It would be a disservice, however, not to point out that Western civilization appears, as Anne Wilson Schaef has argued,[4] to be an intrinsically addictive society. Our personal and collective tendency to grasp for things that bring immediate pleasure and escape or avoid things that bring displeasure is written into the very code and fabric of our culture.

Let's face it; Western civilization thrives on our addiction to materialism. Can you imagine what might happen if, overnight, we all became deeply fulfilled and happy, and we lost our frantic need for the newer, bigger, or shinier to give us momentary pleasure? Well the upside would likely be a transformed and peaceful society, but the stock markets would crash within weeks and either completely transform or die within a few years.

How does this relate to relationships? Simply this: relationships have largely become like everything else in our culture – commodities. We seek them for the pleasure they bring, but in the absence of a deeper and non-grasping appreciation for them, they tend to be viewed as good only so long as we perceive them as "making us happy." Once that stops, many begin looking elsewhere for the next fix.

This deeply ingrained tendency is perhaps the greatest impediment to our personal happiness and fulfillment, and it profoundly impacts our relationships. The antidote: conscious living and conscious relationships.

4) The Second Face of Marriage

There is a second side to marriage that is pervasive, takes up most of a couple's time, yet is rarely formally recognized or addressed. I often suggest to couples that marriage (whether legal or common-law) is like a coin – there are two sides to it. A couple is drawn together out of attraction, they dance the waltz of intimacy, form an emotional bond of love, and then decide to commit to each other because they have each found that special person with whom they want to

---

4. Anne Wilson-Schaef (1987). When Society Becomes An Addict, HarperCollins, NY.

share their lives. The bond of love and companionship is what brings people together; this is the first side of the relationship coin. However…

> *The moment a couple marries or otherwise moves in together, the coin flips, revealing the second side – it is also a business relationship.*

Sound cold or formal? Have doubts? Ask anyone who has recently divorced or is in the midst of one and you'll likely get an earful of just how much of a business marriage is. We go to city hall for a "marriage license" not a declaration of love, and marriage is, after all, defined as "a legal contract that creates kinship."

Marriage is both an emotional bond, and a socio-economic contract, a business if you will, and both have an equal effect on the overall experience of the union. Unlike commercial business relationships, however, the business aspect of a marriage goes largely unrecognized or at least unacknowledged, and this helps set the stage for marital decline. Why?

A typical couple views their marriage as a bond of love and then proceeds to focus almost all of their attention on the 'busyness' of doing life together. They don't do this intentionally but the demands of the business side of relationships have immediate and easily recognized consequences – try not showing up for work or paying the rent and see what happens – whereas the consequences of not protecting and nurturing the emotional bond are usually delayed, subtle, and insidiously cumulative.

> *Romantic love is like a garden, a beautiful and sacred place created by two people to share – most couples begin well by planting for the future, but then neglect it and let it go to seed.*

I often remind distressed couples early in counselling that, assuming they sleep about eight hours per night, they have roughly 112 hours of awake-time each week. Then I ask them how many hours per week they devote to one-on-one quality time with each other. By quality time I mean time spent doing the sort of things they once did when they first began to date, things that help them feel close and appreciated. When the question is asked, most couples glance at each other uncomfortably and then return a vague answer of "One or two hours…maybe." Can any love really endure such neglect?

When asked to account for the rest of their time, the irony becomes apparent; adding up all the time they spend on the business side of the marriage most people in a marriage can easily account for 60 to 70 hours per week. This includes such things as time spent working to bring in money, commuting, attending to domestic tasks (e.g., shopping, cleaning house, laundry, yard work, tending to children etc). Think about that – 60 or 70 hours per week tending to a poorly defined and largely ignored side of marriage and only a few hours on the very thing that brought them together. Is it any wonder that marriages begin to stagnate and couples grow apart after only a few years?

> *Dee's Advice: If we put as much effort and passion into our relationships as we tend to put into our careers, we're bound to succeed.*

Over time, a gap forms between the ideal of the marriage and its reality. This creates tension, a feeling of dissatisfaction that is a wake-up call for some, but something to be avoided for others. When one assumes love is forever and the marriage is a life-long commitment, the thought that something is going wrong after only a few years can triggered feeling of failure and fear, and is often too difficult for couples to talk about. What do they do then?

Well, some decide to have a child or another child in the

hope that it will fix things; some just get busier and focus on careers, home improvements, child care, and/or material acquisitions; others just numb out through the distraction of television and other addictions. Over time the gaps between fantasy and reality and between the partners widens, and this usually leads to deeper dissatisfaction.

Because most couples do not have an agreed-upon exit strategy, the prospect of separation and divorce can be quite frightening and it is easy to feel stuck in an unhappy marriage. Too fearful to separate yet too young to give up on infatuation and passion, is it any wonder why so many marital partners have affairs? This brings us to the fifth factor in the demise of marriage.

5) The Reality – Fantasy Gap

As mentioned earlier, it's quite natural to fantasize about a new love in the moments after our first encounter, often before words are exchanged. Who hasn't wondered what someone we are drawn to is like? Who hasn't had pleasant anticipations once that first date is made, and afterward, when things have gone well, who doesn't imagine the next date? It's a natural thing to do, but overdone, it can start a process that has disastrous effects.

When we fantasize early in a relationship, we tend to imagine being with our partners in ways that bring pleasure. We often start imagining vacations and other fun adventures with people we date, linger on fantasies of passionate lovemaking and so forth. This sort of fantasy is benign if it is infrequent, well informed by reality, and does not project too far into the future. In fact, it can give rise to positive intentions and effective actions that nurture the union and help keep it fresh and growing.

The more risky kind of fantasy is that which projects into the future to imagine the life you want to share with the other person. Fantasizing about events that haven't actually taken place is risky because it creates false memory traces. It may sound like simplistic pop-psychology, but I believe it to be largely true that the mind has a difficult time distinguishing between things we clearly imagine and those that have actually taken place. This is especially true if the imagined events are accompanied by strong emotions, either pleasant or unpleasant.

Fantasizing conflicts with your partner is very damaging and humorously captured by Mark Twain when he said...

My life has been filled with terrible misfortunes, most of which have never happened" ~ Mark Twain.

This sort of negative fantasy – having conversations (i.e., arguments) in your head with your partner – is a way of practicing conflict and creating memory traces that form a net of unpleasant expectations. Once formed, your partner only has to look at you the wrong way or start a sentence that sounds too familiar, and you may feel emotionally triggered. Then the fight is on. Many couples that I see in therapy have created webs so extensive that they cannot have a civil conversation about the weather.

It is also true, however, that fantasizing excessively about perfect romantic evenings or adventurous escapes that are not followed through in the flesh can be damaging. Why? Because they are not real and can lead to creating a relationship fantasy that, over time, may have less and less basis in your physical reality.

I've worked with many people who were grief-stricken over an ended relationship. Upon exploration, they often discover that the lost relationship was toxic to them and that they didn't even like the person who left them. They were, however, in deep grief over the loss of the person and relationships they had created in their mind.

Grief over the loss of the relationship fantasy is often greater than grief for loss of one's partner.

The more we fantasize about our partner and the relationship, the more we create a virtual impression of who and what we are involved with. This not only misinforms our actions toward the real thing, but it can make us blind to reality. What I believe happens with many couples is this: as the true nature of the relationship changes in undesirable ways (e.g., the quality of the love bond is compromised by neglect), the virtual relationship expands and begins to have greater influence over the overall perceptions of how things are going. Usually this fantasy is a product of our ideals and desires and a gap grows wider between it and the real deal.

As the difference between the dream-ideal and the relationship's reality grows, it becomes harder to ignore it or assume that things will just work out. At a critical point, one or both people recognize that the reality of their union is so far off the mark and that the dream may never be realized. When this happens, some couples mobilize and tackle the issues head on, but far too many avoid it out of fear. Like a dirty diaper, though, avoiding it only makes things worse.

This is when the big compromises are most likely to be made. The feared immediate consequences of separation and divorce often hold sway over the delayed cost of giving up things that are fundamentally important to us. When core values, needs, or desires are compromised, the relationship becomes a farce, something that will make the participants lives smaller and poorer. This is when people engage in habitual distractions (e.g., watching TV too much, spending more time at work or with the guys, focusing too much on the children) and begin to look outside of the relationship for what they are missing.

The time course may vary from couple to couple but the process is likely to be the same. Of the couples that find themselves in this sort of crisis, some will try to work through it themselves, some will opt for marital counselling, and some will numb themselves to things further and live on in quiet desperation. Of those who try to fix the problem, some will fail because things have slipped too far for too long, and those who are courageous enough, desperate enough, or evolved enough to end the relationship will do so. The rest will join the ranks of those soldiering on in an unfulfilling union.

Here's a sobering thought I'll reiterate: if about half of marriages end in divorce today, what percentage of couples live on in quiet desperation or at least make due with what they have?

Does it have to be this way? Can the pitfalls of modern marriage be avoided? I believe so.

A Challenging Suggestion

What if something compelled couples to be more conscious of how well they were tending to both the emotional, and the business aspects of their union? What if something strongly encouraged them to remain aware of what was working and not working and obligated them to discuss these and negotiate needed changes on a regular basis? What if both partners were in a situation wherein they knew either one could opt out of a union without legal complications or undue financial burden? What if each knew that nothing bound them but their continued desire to remain together? This is the concept of the One Year Marriage.

Living such a relationship would call for courage of heart and a deep commitment to the love that binds you with your beloved. It would also require confidence in your ability to go it alone if need be, and an internal sense of well-being and security. Only the reckless or foolhardy would enter such a union without ensuring they continue to remain on their personal life paths and retain a viable degree of financial independence. A union that is held together only by the desire of two people to be together would strongly motivate both to retain a viable level of personal sovereignty.

That takes us back to that visualization in the preface of the book – two sovereign rulers of their own kingdoms, a king and a queen if you will, each independent and powerful in their own right, sharing their lives through love yet never relinquishing their claims to their own realms.

In the coming chapters I will to argue that the One Year Marriage holds promise to unite people just that way; by helping them retain their individualities, the things that make them desired and special in the first place, while encouraging a conscious nurturing of the relationship.

Chapter 2

Marriage Redefined: Towards a New Paradigm for Love and Romance

"There's only one way to have a happy marriage and as soon as I learn what it is, I'll get married again." ~ Clint Eastwood.

Thinking Outside the Box – The One Year Marriage

As I shared in the preface, the concept of the One Year Marriage came to me during one of those insightful moments of thinking outside of the box. Such thinking is freer, less restricted by assumptions about how something must be done, and is a hot item in the business world for good reason: liberated thinking drives innovation. It's the sort of thinking Steve Jobs was revered for.

The core question that gave rise to this book was this: Is there a way to prevent the deterioration in love and happiness that the majority of marriages fall prey to? On that California beach that day, an "outside-the-box" solution was The One Year Marriage.

As much as it might sound otherwise, I'm not suggesting we completely reinvent marriage – a OYM is still two people coming together (perhaps more if you are polyamorous) to share their lives in love and happiness, and there is a great deal of flexibility with which it can be applied. The OYM model can be embraced completely, or features can be used to modify a current or planned conventional marriage. Once you have a concrete knowledge of the model and the rationale for its design, you'll be able to decide for yourself what features might work for you.

Why risk something as important as a marriage by trying something so radical and new? Because you have nothing to lose – there is no risk. At any time the two of you can mutually agree to convert a OYM to whatever you wish or simply toss the contract out the widow. More important, you may well gain what you deeply desire in a marriage, and at the very least, you're guaranteed to learn a lot about your selves and each other.

So what exactly am I proposing? Simply this: *that couples consciously approach their relationship commitments as mutually negotiated one-year agreements that, if not renewed at the anniversary, automatically dissolve according to agreed-upon terms.*

Does that seem emotionally cowardly or unromantic to you? Then riddle me this… which takes more faith and courage – a relationship wherein your partner is legally and perpetually bound to you with potentially serious financial and emotional penalties for breaking the union – or one in which he or she can walk away without undue complications? Which is more romantic – two people bound together by legal, economic, and emotional obligation, or two people bound solely by their love and desire to remain together? I'm an idealist romantic at heart; I'll go with the latter in each case.

If the courageously romantic twist of the OYM doesn't appeal to you, consider this: what if it could actually help you and your partner to grow as individuals, and to support each other in that growth. Contrast that with the reality of most conventional marriages wherein growth is too often perceived to be a threat.

Do you doubt that last statement? Can you imagine the reaction that most conventionally married people would have if their spouse informed them they wanted to take six months off and travel…alone. Aside from the expected concerns about what's happening and how they will manage the practical side of things, how many married people do you know who would be emotionally prepared to handle that and be able to support his or her spouse in the venture?

What if a OYM could help you and your partner cultivate a sense of deeply rooted security that freed you both of fear and clinging? What if it helped create a greater sense of mutual appreciation and respect? Remember the image of the king and queen, each sovereign over a kingdom of their own yet sharing a life? What if a OYM could help you create just such a union? I believe it can.

Is a OYM practical? Most assuredly so, and much easier to create and maintain than you might think. We'll cover the details of how to create and nurture a viable OYM later. For now, let's take a closer look at some of the benefits.

The Benefits

The benefits discussed here are general and apply to both men and women. How they may apply differently to women and men is addressed in chapters three and four. Some of the benefits presented are closely related and the distinctions between them may seem arbitrary. If you find yourself puzzled by this, it may be best not to try to differentiate them at this point.

Clarity and Conscious Living

An important benefit of the OYM is greater clarity for you and your partner about what each wants from the relationship, and about how you and your partner agree to honour those desires. It also facilitates conscious, agreed-upon change over time.

The OYM compels us to be very specific about our likes,

dislikes, desires, and intentions. Most people talk about these issues in the early stages of a relationship, and many continue to talk about them throughout a relationship, but the talk often amounts to lip service. All too often when something disagreeable happens between partners, they broach the matter in the form of a complaint, only to meet resistance; their partners most often go on the defensive and fire off a complaint or two of their own in response. The result is nothing other than hurt feelings and frustration.

Over time, this breakdown in communication can result in a near complete disconnect from what each other wants. Even when couples do sort out their differences when they conflict, they rarely dig deeper into root causes or come up with a plan to prevent repeats of the issue. Perhaps more tragic is when someone chooses not to address an issue and hopes or assumes that things will somehow work out. This road often leads to compromising one's integrity and happiness to keep the peace.

Example: Carolyn was first drawn to Patrick because he was a fun guy to be around. Everywhere he went he knew someone and people greeted him with a wide smile. Dating meant three to four nights a week spent at one pub or party or another. She knew life with Patrick would never be dull.

When they married, Carolyn assumed Pat would cut down on his partying and begin cultivating deeper, quieter moments to share. She still liked to have fun but after three years of marriage, she realized that nothing had changed from when they were first dating. Pat was not 'progressing' as she had expected. She declined to go out, hoping he would remain home with her, but he'd go anyway. She tried talking to him about it but he laughed and told her his lifestyle was what she said she'd liked about him.

Carolyn suppressed her objections but after four years, she became increasingly unhappy. She pressed Pat again for change, for them to begin enjoying other things. When her protests could not be suppressed by his charm and jokes, Pat became angry and verbally aggressive. She was frightened by this and lapsed into silence again.

Carolyn continued to gently broach the issue and tried other ways to get Patrick to 'grow up' and take a more serious approach to life, but each time it was met with flippant remarks or verbal aggression. It felt to her as though he would leave if she pressed too hard. It was only after eight years of marriage that she came to realize Patrick was in another relationship that he held more dearly than their marriage – his relationship with alcohol. Pat was an alcoholic and Carolyn had compromised herself by adjusting to his lifestyle.

Sound a little dramatic? It isn't – that is a relatively mild example of the ways I've known people to compromise themselves in marriages by becoming numb to their true needs or otherwise not having a reliable means to negotiate change. That was also an example of how the assumption of permanence entraps people in unions where one partner can exert undue control within the relationship. I'll address that more in chapter three.

The cooperative and yearly process of creating a OYM agreement ensures partners are more conscious of what each wants from the relationship. The automatic and obstacle-free dissolution of the agreement (hence the relationship) that is ever present and mere months away, creates a compelling mandate for both partners to honour the accord. The result is remaining conscious of what has been identified as important to each other and how that is being honoured.

Conscious living is effective living; it is being aware of

what is really happening around us and the options we're presented with each day for dealing with it, and it's making informed choices. Unconscious living is like wandering around not knowing quite where you are, what you want, and not knowing how you'd get it if you did. It can mean wandering aimlessly with no place to go.

That may be a nice way to do a vacation, but as a lifestyle it leads to boredom, addictions, and regrets at the end of one's days. Conscious living is knowing where you are, where you want to go, and having a clear path to get there. Doesn't approaching a marriage consciously make sense?

Greater Awareness

Closely related to clarity and consciousness is greater ongoing awareness of your own needs and desires. The OYM compels us to evaluate what is working and not working in the relationship and to be aware of what may or may not be working for our partner. Whether ongoing or periodic, this sort of evaluation is rarely done in any meaningful way in most contemporary marriages. That is part of the presumption of permanence that was discussed in the previous chapter.

To reiterate, the practice of formalizing conscious agreements to help ensure the health and happiness of the relationship is exceedingly rare in contemporary marriage. Couples tend to go on faith that they will honour each other's needs, and many feel that to do otherwise (e.g., to formalize things) is a sign of mistrust. In actuality, it is just a recognition and acknowledgment of reality. It is quite normal and expected that people will neglect a task when the consequences of doing so are vague and delayed. This is especially true when there are competing demands for time and attention that have immediate consequences.

Take the way we mind our health, for example. It is

entirely too common for people to eat too much or choose unhealthy foods, to not get enough exercise or rest, to smoke, to drink too much, etc. The main killers of adults in the Western world today are largely a function of lifestyle choices. So why do so many people choose to compromise their health and thereby lessen the length and quality of their lives? We're hard wired that way, I'm afraid.

The immediate consequences of a behaviour, whether positive or negative, will tend to have a greater influence on our choices than delayed consequences, regardless how serious the latter may be. This is true of all members of the animal kingdom.

The above is a well-documented psychological phenomenon, and it's particularly robust when the delayed consequences are only possibilities. Hence, the momentary pleasure of inhaling tobacco has a much greater influence on a smoker's choice to smoke than the real possibility that it **might** lead to an early and painful death – 20 years from now. The thought of enjoying an extra helping of cake or a greasy meal can have a greater influence in the moment of decision than the knowledge that it will make losing that extra 10 pounds even harder. We can overcome this natural tendency of course, but it takes learned and practiced skills (i.e., self-management skills) to do so.

When it comes to putting in the time and care to cultivate our marriages, things are no different. There are just so many competing demands for our time and attention. Many demands from the business side of our relationships have immediate, observable consequences (employment, car payments, rent, electric bills, shopping, cleaning, etc). Without a compelling reason to remain aware of each other's desires and how well the relationship is working; without motivation to put in the time and energy to honour these, such considerations are easily relegated to the back burner where they can remain dangerously long.

Accountability

Accountability is critical for most human endeavours. For many, it carries the negative nuance of being "held accountable" which is usually the prelude to some form of punishment. Accountability here, however, is simply using the process and structure of the OYM to support both partners in following through with how they have decided to honour each other and cultivate their love.

If you and your partner have mutually agreed to something in the marriage, then presumably you'll both want to follow through on it. For now, let's assume that you and your partner have just agreed that you need to work on a few things in the marriage. Maybe you have to curb your spending and your partner needs to find a job. Perhaps your partner has agreed to pick up after him- or her-self more and you've acknowledged that you haven't been taking care of your health as well as you could. What do you think the most likely thing to prevent the two of you from working on those issues would be?

Let me digress a moment. Coaching is a vibrant business these days and for good reason: it works. People hire coaches to help them do everything from losing weight to becoming more successful. The reason isn't that coaches can tell you just what you need to do to reach your dreams (though we often have some solid tips), it's that they provide structure and accountability.

Coaching helps you determine just what you want to accomplish and what changes would make the biggest difference in your life. You set effective goals (i.e., goals that are positive, specific, measurable, and time limited), you set objectives for yourself that will culminate in reaching your goal, and you are held accountable for whether you do what you've said you would do. This accountability is supportive, not punitive, and it accounts for at least 50% of coaching's effectiveness.

It is this kind of accountability that the OYM provides. The negotiated marital agreement is comparable to a set of goals the two of you have decided on. Similarly, the assessment and review of the agreement as the anniversary approaches is analogous to reviewing how you have fared in your objectives with your coach. The renegotiation of a new agreement is analogous to fine tuning your objectives and the plan to meet them. In essence, the OYM brings this core strength of coaching into your relationship to help ensure your success.

There is another aspect of accountability in the OYM that does have a negative vibe but it is positive nevertheless. When it comes time to review how things have been going (I recommend doing this monthly rather than near the anniversary date) each of you will be held accountable in a subtle way for how you have honoured your side of the agreement. If your partner has fallen short on something important to you, how he or she is willing to accept responsibility for that and act in good faith is very telling about the integrity of your partner and the viability of the relationship.

It is common for marital partners to make promises to each other that they expect not to keep just for the sake of getting something they want, even if that is only to appease their partner at the time. Others intend to keep their agreements but decide not to honour them and then play games to avoid accountability.

One game is the "I'm sorry" recording that gets played over more times than a top 10 single. Another is the "yes but" game of endless excuses. The worst game of all is hardball – "if you don't like it, leave." Any such game play is an indicator of a serious problem in your partner's willingness or ability to carry his or her weight in a healthy relationship and the structure and process of the OYM can help you identify that sooner rather later.

Perhaps the most important form of accountability the OYM offers is your accountability to yourself. By declaring your desires and intentions, affirming your boundaries, stating how you have agreed to honour your partner's needs, and putting this all in writing, you are creating a benchmark to assess your own continued integrity in the marriage. Are you honouring your obligations? Are you holding your partner to his or hers? If not, the OYM process will make it very clear and obvious.

The benefit of that is it can help prevent you from compromising yourself in the marriage. When you, or your partner, are compromised in any significant way because of your relationship, your union is in jeopardy, often without immediate awareness. The OYM helps ensure continued, conscious, and mutually shared awareness of the relationship's realities.

Constructive Insecurity

From a slightly different angle, a OYM makes effective, constructive use of insecurity. We tend to favour the 'honour system' when it comes to our partnership agreements and as noble as that may seem, it is a source of much suffering in marriages.

Take a job situation for example. Let's say you hire someone to do a job and that person promises to work hard and give you good value for your money. Let's also say you take his word on it and put nothing in place to track his performance or otherwise hold him accountable. How do you think that person will perform over time? Chances are, his performance will start out strong and then slack off, and when there is no feedback or consequence to that, his performance will slacken even more. Before too long, you're not happy with your employee and your employee is bored with his job because it's not challenging enough. This tendency to do as little as possible to meet external demands (call it an innate laziness or an efficiency imperative) is a robust feature of human behaviour and we are all vulnerable to it. People pleasers and Type-A's may appear to be exceptions, but if you examine their behaviour closely, you'll see even they exhibit the tendency, all be it in more subtle ways.

Contrast that with a contracted employee. You enter into a contract for a stated, limited period with clear expectations for a certain level of performance. Even if you do not provide regular feedback on how well the employee is doing, imagine how his/her work would fare over the year. Experience would suggest that it would start out high, taper off a little with time, but not too much, and then pick up again as the end of the year approaches.

The net result is consistently higher diligence, performance, and a happier employee. Why happier? Because we need a degree of challenge to keep our interests alive, and because day-to-day experience and research suggest that when we have a limited amount of time remaining to take part in something, we tend to appreciate that endeavour more and are motivated to make the most of it.[5] It's a win-win outcome from simply formalizing the impermanence of the job.

In a similar way, the time-limited nature of the OYM encourages greater consistency and diligence in working to keep the partnership alive and well, and enhances our appreciation of it. Could a partner with more financial

---

5. See www.sciencedaily.com/releases/2009/01/090112110104.htm

resources or social power abuse this, much like an unscrupulous employer could abuse it? Certainly, but you will know it quickly and remain aware of it. Then, should you decide to stay in a fundamentally abusive relationship, you will do so consciously. That may be a bad choice for you in the long run, but it is entirely within your rights as a sovereign being, and at the end of the day it will be on you, as much as your abusive partner.

Good Business Partnership

The OYM effectively recognizes and honours the business side of a union by formalizing it. Why is this important? Imagine two people, who know and like each other, come up with a great idea for a new business. They enter into this commercial venture with what little cash they have, high hopes, and good intentions. Business agreement? "Nah, we don't need that, we're friends and we like each other. We'll agree to always do right by each other." Anyone with any business background knows the folly of this and will predict that the venture will most likely fail. If it doesn't, then one or both partners will probably wish it had. For those readers without an appreciation for business, think about these scenarios.

- The business becomes wildly successful and there is great cash flow, only the two of you have different ideas about what to do with the money.

- Business is great but you find yourself doing most of the work while your partner is spending most of the profits.

- Your partner decides to hire a family member without your consultation and consent.

- The business is doing poorly and you want out but you and your partner cannot agree on a buy out price.

- Someone you detest and know you could not work with offers your partner a good sum of money for his half of the business.

- You decide you don't like working with your partner and you want out but your partner refuses to buy you out and threatens legal action if you try to sell your half.

These are but a few simple but realistic problems that a small partnership with no business agreement could face – and rather quickly. The potential problems are legion. In fact, if this partnership ever needed a bank loan for the business and the bank discovered it had no business agreement or had one without an exit strategy, they'd have a better chance of winning the lottery than getting the loan.

The short of if it is this: in a business partnership you need the support of a solid, fair, agreement to guide both parties and ensure things are done right, when circumstances might compel one or more of them to do otherwise. Why should it be any different with the most important business relationship you might form in this life – a marriage?

A good partnership agreement, like one used in a OYM, is a healthy way to formally recognize the business side of your union and create healthy guidelines by which to conduct yourselves (i.e., honour each other). Remember the problems generated by assumptions and fantasy discussed in chapter one? The OYM agreement is a good way to ground the two of you in reality.

A solid marital agreement can ensure that: (1) you and your beloved enter into the partnership with a clear, mutually agreed-upon set of expectations; (2) your expectations are up-front with no hidden agendas or surprise clauses; (3) you're both assured equal power and say in the partnership; (4) your personal assets are shielded in the event of partnership failure; and (5) there is a sunset clause and predetermined exit strategy that protects the best interests of both of you, and that clause automatically takes effect at 12:01 am on the anniversary of the agreement.

Some people have a problem with the last item – automatic termination. It is, however, an essential feature, largely responsible for keeping the quality of your relationship on the front burner. Many of the benefits of the OYM hinge on its power to motivate both partners to honour themselves and each other in the best possible ways.

Why a year? Why not two or five? A year is perfect and powerful. A calendar year is one complete cycle of the seasons, a turning of the wheel and it is more or less the maximum amount of time that people seem to be able to think ahead in a way that is motivational. If a couple needs to re-evaluate their marriage in two or three years, you are likely to see the marital health put on the back burner for more than half that time. "Hey honey, do we redo the agreement this August or next?" "Next year, Darling. Not to worry, there's plenty of time." Having a set date that demands a renewal that is no further away than 12 months to the second and counting, is magnitudes more powerful and effective than longer periods.

It may seem burdensome at first to have to renegotiate and renew a marital contract every year, but it doesn't have to be. Once one is in place, it can be used to guide your review and evaluation and can simply be updated to reflect changes you both agree to. Legal costs in most jurisdictions would also be minimal to nothing since once a binding contract is set up, the format can be used repeatedly without legal counsel.

I will write more about the nuts and bolts and legalities of OYM agreements in chapter seven, but how about a quick check in. How are you doing with all this so far? Here's a friendly challenge: if you feel resistance to the notion of entering into this sort of partnership, make a few mental notes on your thoughts. Better still; write them out. Chapter six will help you explore these in detail – you may learn a lot about yourself and your partner.

Minding Your Own Business – Retaining Sovereignty

So is this just a male-oriented scheme that panders to the desire of some men to have a relationship with all the benefits of commitment (e.g., your partner isn't open to the sexual advances of other men) with a clean getaway? Who would really benefit from living the One Year Marriage? Well, it turns out men and women are equal beneficiaries, both economically and emotionally, and one of the core benefits is the retention of personal sovereignty.

The idea that two people come together to make one in marriage is rather quaint, but it's appallingly dysfunctional – and damaging. It promotes the idea that two independent people come together in a marriage and become dependent on each other for their identity and material well being. It is a model of assimilation, and as with the Borg in the Star Trek TV and movie phenomenon, each partner's individual distinctiveness is to be assimilated to serve the collective. This is the notion that encouraged women to give up their careers and birth surnames in deference to those of their husbands. Men have been serious losers under this model as well, as will be discussed further in chapter four.

Some research[6] suggests that people overly committed to their relationships, whose self-esteem is affected by how well their relationship is doing (something called "relationship-contingent self-esteem") are much more prone to strong emotional reactions not just to relationships ending but to perceived threats to them. Clinical experience has taught me that this often results in anxious and hostile reactions to innocent spouse behaviours, and readily leads to attempts to control the partner.

Example: Julie met Jon at a community function and

6. (cf. Science daily, December 3, 2008)

they began dating right away. She found Jon to be more giving and attentive that any partner she'd dated before and within two months they decided that he would move in with her. At first, he was amazingly helpful with keeping the household going – doing repairs, minor renovations, and pitching in just about any way he could. Julie thought she'd finally met her prince in lustrous armour. Before long, however, Jon began to show another side to his personality.

He began questioning her about her coworkers and objecting to her twice-monthly girls-night out with her friends. Whenever the phone would ring, he seemed to always be nearby as she spoke and asked whom she'd been talking to. It was an annoyance that escalated when Jon was laid off from his seasonal work. That's when he began to want her to account for her time outside of the home.

When driving, if Julie turned her head and there happened to be a man in the direction she glanced, Jon would demand to know who he was and how she knew him. On one occasion, when she denied even seeing the man he was referring to, he stopped his truck and threatened to drive back to confront him unless she told him. Julie discovered that her prince was a troll in disguise and it took six painful months to extricate herself from the nightmare.

Although Jon may have had other issues that made him vulnerable to becoming emotionally dependent on Julie, the result of emotional enmeshment with one's partner is similar for most people, though usually less dramatic. This very corrosive process can leave one or both partners feeling trapped in something they cannot live with or without.

A OYM compels autonomy if done correctly, which itself can   effectively   prevent   economic   and   emotional enmeshment. For those predisposed to emotional dependency (as Jon was in the above example), the OYM process is bound to bring that tendency to the forefront of awareness and challenge the individual to come to terms with it. The outcome of that would be to stimulate personal and interpersonal growth and, in turn, lead to greater autonomy and self-esteem.

Similarly, some research has found that ending a relationship can result in significant changes in self-concept.[7] This is thought to be due to blending one's own self with that of one's partner. The implications of this are simple for our purposes: the greater the blending of self-concepts, the greater the loss of one's individuality. From the perspective of Western psychology, a reduction in clarity of self-concept is not a good thing.

Not that a shared concept of "we" in a relationship is a bad thing – on the contrary it's beautiful on many levels; however, this can be cultivated and enjoyed without the loss of one's sense of self. In fact, without a solid individual identity, a collective identity cannot be fully realized or appreciated. Living the OYM is a means for women and men to retain a strong sense of who they are, what their personal life path is, while cultivating and taking pleasure in a healthy sense of who they are as a couple.

Remember the study mentioned in chapter one that reported the seven-year-itch was becoming the three-year-glitch? I hinted there was a healthy aspect to this and here it is: I believe the glitch can be a healthy wake-up call for people who have lost something important somewhere along the road of relationship bliss. That something is their sense of personal life-path and sovereignty.

As alluded to in chapter one, we are as a rule, happiest

7. (cf, Science Daily, March 12, 2010)

and at our best when we are aligned with a personal path in life, a purpose that is based on our deepest values and beliefs. Such purpose guides us toward personal growth, integration, and meaning, which are the foundations of deep fulfillment. The purpose can be grand or simple, but without it, we tend to feel dissatisfied and our lives lack deeper meaning.

How does this relate to relationships? Simple – anyone who focuses on a joint life-path or purpose with a partner at the expense of his or her personal one, will become dissatisfied at a deep, visceral level. When that happens, the thing that seemed to bring so much purpose and happiness at first (i.e., the relationship) will fall short of our needs. Glitch! Ironically, the glitch is not necessarily in the relationship itself, but in the unrealistic expectation that a joint life purpose can replace our personal one and then letting the latter fade.

It's not an either/or issue by any means; having a joint mission with a beloved is important to the life and vitality of any partnership and can be the source of profound satisfaction and joy. Maintaining a personal purpose, however, is ground zero – the Holy Grail – and without it, all else will fail.

A different model of relationships can be seen in many ancient wisdom traditions: two people come together to make three – you, me, and us. This is a model of integration and is the philosophical foundation of the OYM; two independent people come together to form a union of love and healthy interdependence.

Certainly, it is possible to retain one's sense of self and personal mission in a traditional marriage, but it is exceedingly difficult and rare. However, when forced independence may be only 12 months away and counting, as with a OYM, very few would give up their careers, dreams, identities, personal financial solvency, or compromise anything important for the sake of the "us."

That may sound like a lack of commitment to a relationship, but it's not – it is simply maintaining commitment to one's own life path, which should never need to be compromised. The final outcome of that is a happier individual who has a real life to share with his or her beloved, rather than a dissatisfied individual who clings to his or her partner in co-dependent angst.

I will go into this in more detail in the next two chapters because there are some ways that the retention of sovereignty can benefit men and women differently.

Personal Growth and Happiness

The OYM strongly promotes retaining our dreams and aspirations and by that it supports our individual growth. It obliges us to maintain our individual identities so we can 'go it alone' again if need be. A nice side effect of that is that we are then bound to continue to be the interesting characters our partners fell in love with. It compels us to mind our personal financial viability as we may well find ourselves flying solo after the next anniversary (theoretically at least). This encourages personal financial responsibility and solvency in both partners, and by direct consequence, collective financial well-being.

I've been privy to the plight of many individuals who were financially viable when single, but who became collectively bankrupt when married. As a rule, two people who continue to manage their own affairs well are better able to contribute to a collective financial life than two people who experience financial enmeshment and diffusion.

Embracing Impermanence

Perhaps one of the more profound ways the OYM can

benefit the more evolved or spiritually inclined of us is by encouraging recognition of impermanence. In the Buddhist tradition, we are advised to be aware of and embrace impermanence as an inevitable fact of life. Each of us will lose everything and everyone we cherish at some point in our lifetime, even if only at death, and there is great wisdom in embracing this.

When I first learned of this principle, my immediate reaction was to reject the notion as negative and morose – who wants to live life with the expectation of pervasive, inviolable, inescapable loss? The wisdom in it, as I learned after years of resistance, lies in what that acknowledgment does for us – put simply, by recognizing the temporary nature of everything, our appreciation for what we have increases. Though commonly espoused in the wisdom traditions, this concept has received scientific validation as well.[8] More important, it is evident in our everyday experiences.

Have you ever noticed a tendency to take special pleasure in the last few morsels of a delicious meal? Assuming you're not satiated, those final tidbits can be the most appreciated and tastiest. On a more profound scale, when we appreciate something and recognize that we have a limited time to enjoy it, we're inclined to pay more attention to it, relish in its experience and appreciate the joy it brings.

Most of us have heard tales of people who, after a near-death experience, make profound lifestyle changes and begin to live a more authentic and satisfying life. An intensely effective Buddhist exercise is to meditate on one's own death and come to a place of compassionate acceptance. The outcome is a richer appreciation for every moment of the life we have. Similarly, contemplating the death of a loved one

8. (e.g., J.L. Kurtz, Science Daily, Jan 13, 2009)

can increase our appreciation for that person and compel us to attend more to the quality of our time with our beloved. What relationship would not improve from that?

If you're like most people, the concept of embracing impermanence may feel threatening at first and certainly unromantic. The good news is that, as it applies to the OYM, the impermanence is much more gentle and palatable; since it is built in, codified in the automatic dissolution of the union, it serves to remind each partner of the unavoidably limited time with the other. By that it can cultivate a deeper appreciation for the relationship and help ensure that your time together, the health of your union, remains a high priority. What's more, the marriage is renewable as many times as the two of you care to renew it, perhaps for as long as you both live.

The anniversary can then become a celebration of life shared, an earnest reflection and appraisal of the marriage, and, if desired, a time of renewal and commitment – for one more year. Always for just one more turn of the wheel, one more year. The union between two lovers thereby falls into sync with the natural rhythms of life, much like the seasons.

Masculine and Feminine Essence

An interesting way to look at marital relationships is from the perspective of masculine and feminine energies or tendencies. It's a perspective that we are intuitively aware of and it has been written about extensively in both ancient and modern times. John Gray has written some wonderful books using the Martian and Venusian metaphor to explore these divergences to help couples come to recognize, accept, and work with their differences.[9] David Deida has written books that more directly address the differences in male and female

---

9. John Gray (1992) Men are from Mars, Women are from Venus. Harper Collins, NY.

essence and how these play out in one-on-one relationships and at the sociological level.[10]

Keep in mind that masculine and feminine essence is not synonymous with male and female genders since each gender embodies both tendencies to some extent. However, one or the other dominates in most people. At the risk of sounding old school, it appears that most women are dominated by the characteristics and tendencies of the feminine, and most men are dominated by the masculine.

We can draw on our subordinate energies, of course – women can embody the qualities of the masculine when needed or desired, and men can embody the feminine, but the dominant one will come more naturally and effortlessly. If that still seems sexist to you, perhaps referring to these differences as Type-I and Type-II tendencies may help. If you define yourself outside of the traditional categories of male or female, you will still observe these characteristics in some blended form, as they are essential human qualities.

So how does this play out in relationships and how is this relevant to the OYM? Male and female essence is akin to Yin / Yang of the Taoist tradition – they form two halves of a whole. Each has its characteristic strengths and weaknesses; but, where one is weak, the other is strong. By themselves, they are incomplete when expressed in someone's life, within a family, or even at a societal level; each one itself, in the absence of its counterpart, is likely to lead to an imbalance.

There are many facets of this, but one core difference between the masculine and the feminine is in the focus each has when it comes to relationships. Put simply, masculine essence tends to value structure, boundaries, and rules. The dark side of this is that it can lead to excessive efforts to

10. David Deida (1995). Intimate Communion: Awakening Your Sexual Essence. Health Communications, Deerfield Beach, FL.

control if unbalanced and unchecked. The positive aspect is that it is the primary driving force behind the ideal of justice for all. The feminine values harmonious relationships and nurturance. The dark side, when unbalanced and unchecked, can be social and emotional chaos. The positive aspect is the main driving force behind providing for the needs of all.

These differences can be seen in parenting approaches. Ever wonder why the homemakers of yesteryear used to say, "Wait until your father gets home"? They can also been seen at a societal level. From this perspective, a country like the U.S.A., which has a strong and punitive law-and-order mentality, has a relatively weak social support network in comparison to other developed nations. It could be said to be suffering from an excess of masculine influence. By contrast, some European countries, which have strong policies of social care and responsibility but lack boundaries in regard to personal responsibility for self, might be said to be suffering from an excess of feminine influence. Some nations, Canada for example, appear to have a healthy balance of the two, where strong and fair justice systems and an ethos of personal responsibility are complemented by universal health care and good programs in educational and social support.

Suffice it to say that whether one is talking about a society, an organization, or a couple's relationship, both the masculine and feminine aspects get played out and need to be in balance. This is true for same-gender unions as well. One critical way these become expressed is in the two sides of the relationship coin: the business side is very masculine in nature; the emotional bond side is very feminine. So, how does the OYM model help strike a healthy balance?

One of the problems with managing the masculine and feminine sides of a union is that most couples do it unconsciously. People simply enter a union with the best of intentions to share their love and lives without due thought about how to do that. As discussed in chapter one, the business (a.k.a., busyness) side gets most of the attention and the masculine comes to dominate. Before long, the feminine side suffers neglect, and the emotional connection wilts like a spring flower in the summer sun.

The ironic part of this is that if couples initially used the masculine aspect in a conscious way to create a firm agreement with articulated boundaries (e.g., a one-year-marriage contract), it would bring the critical importance of the feminine into the foreground. In other words, "here's an agreement to share our lives for one year that automatically dissolves on the anniversary. The agreement can be renegotiated and renewed if and only if both of us want that, and that will most likely depend on whether we are happy and satisfied with the quality of our love and our lives together."

It's not so much that couples need more masculine energy; they need the careful application of healthy boundaries as a support to ensure fairness and focus. Good fences make good neighbours, so the saying goes, and they make good life-partners. People will sometimes agree to anything in principle but when it comes to delivery, they can be terrible at it.

For couples entering a "lifelong" or even a "year long" agreement, adherence to that agreement cannot be on good faith alone because such pacts generally do not stand the test of time. This is why business interests today don't simply shake on deals; they sign legal contracts and those are what make the deals fair and workable over time. It may be hard to swallow but the same is true of marriages.

In the next two chapters, I will address the ways that a OYM might benefit women and men differently.

Chapter 3

The Feminine Perspective

"Any intelligent woman who reads the marriage contract, and then goes into it, deserves all the consequences." ~ *Isadora Duncan*

What are Women Looking for From Marriage?

This chapter is about what women want from relationships, from love and marriage, and how a One Year Marriage can help them attain their desires. It my be a hard sell for some, but I believe a OYM offers women greater security and satisfaction than its traditional cousin, while at the same time promoting personal growth and sovereignty. It's a win-win, the best of both worlds.

As I pointed out in the last chapter, the OYM model springs from the masculine tendency to strive for rules (guidelines sound nicer), personal sovereignty, and fairness. I suggested that ensuring these formed the foundation of a relationship would support the feminine tendency to cultivate love, harmony, and nurturance.

That may sound like a throwback to the days when men provided the land and house, while women made the home, but keep in mind that those roles, as rigid and limiting as they had been, were largely based on the complementary strengths of the genders. Remember also that the masculine / feminine tendencies I refer to are not quite synonymous with the male / female genders. Both genders have both essences, only in different proportions for most people.

The fact that most men have a predominance of one

essence and women the other is the reason for naming them masculine and feminine essence. As suggested in chapter two, if the terms are troubling, you can substitute Type-I and Type-II energies for them.

So what do women want from marriage? Let's approach this from several levels, starting from the broad lens of sociobiology, and shifting to the metaphysical level of gender essence, and finally ending in the fine distinctions of individual differences.

Sociobiology 101

Sociobiology is a fascinating field that strives to explain social behaviour in terms of its adaptive or evolutionary significance. Why even go here? Because there is good reason to believe that some of the things women find attractive in men and seek in their relationships today have their roots in our early history as a species. Some of these may still hold relevance today, while others may have been rendered irrelevant by modern socio-economic realities. What's more, it appears that some of these innate attractions are not only of no use today; they may actually lead women into bad relationships. Forewarned is forearmed.

As an intellectual tool, sociobiology offers an elegant means to explore and speculate on why animals do what they do, in much the same way the principles of natural and sexual selection help us understand why animals are built the way they are. What follows doesn't necessarily reflect current thought in the field and many of the speculations are my own. It is offered simply as an example of how sociobiology might account for commonly observed female mating strategies.

When speculating about the biological basis for why women seek what they do in men and marriage, it's important to shift our time frame to our pre-civilization roots. I'm referring to the 150,000 to 200,000 years that we lived in small bands of hunter-gatherers of no more than 50 to 100 people. What would influence a woman's mate selection then? Who would have been a great catch? What would she have looked for in a "marriage" way back in the day?

Enter Lucy. She's a 13-year-old member of a small band of hunter-gathers somewhere in Eurasia 70,000 years ago. Her people live close to the earth, never far from the dangers of predators and food shortage. She should have been mated by now and people are beginning to talk, but Lucy is rather particular. She knows the welfare of every member of the band is a community concern, but growing up she'd seen the added security that a good mate (and father) could provide, especially during food shortages and when saber-toothed cats and bears roamed the vicinity. Lucy wants to choose her mate well.

Though she is not consciously aware of it, what Lucy finds attractive in a mate has been determined by what male characteristics helped her female ancestors and their children survive long enough to continue the family line. It was no easy task: between the high risk of carrying a child and later giving birth; high infant mortality; limited life span; and the high demand of caring for a child for years until it could contribute to the band, mating was a high-risk, high-cost venture. It was a testimony to the strength of her matrilineal line and their choices in mates that Lucy was alive to take up her role as an adult.

Since she's about to play the risky game of procreation, what advice would you give Lucy for selecting a mate? We can assume that pairing with a male who will help feed and protect her and their children will help her survive and continue her genetic line, but how will she know him when she sees him, and are there other traits she ought to cue into (i.e., what "fitness indicators" should she look for)?

Put another way, if you were Mother Nature and had to 'program' Lucy to be unconsciously attracted to certain traits in males that would help optimize her genetic success (i.e., maximize the number of children she leaves who live long enough to procreate), what programming would you select? Did it come down to size mattering after all – should she simply seek out the biggest dude in camp?

All things being equal, size might have been a good fitness indicator in the earliest days of our species and, indeed, Lucy is attracted to larger males. However, her (our) task is more complicated than that – size alone is not a reliable indicator of toughness, and doesn't have a close relationship to a man's hunting or fishing skills, or his ability to keep her alive in the face of natural calamities.

She instinctively finds overall health and physical prowess attractive in guys, and is attracted as well to certain personality characteristics like determination, diligence, and unwavering assertiveness. As it turns out, such characteristics were likely predictive of a mate who would protect and provide.[11] Most attractive to Lucy was, however, the way a man carried himself and how well his peers respected him.

Back to the present time for a moment, this is not to say that our female ancestors sought some form of "alpha-male" as a mate. I don't believe true alphas have ever existed among humans – we're simply too complex and socially fluid for such a simple social scheme. However, in early bands of hunter-gatherers, status would likely have been afforded to men in proportion to how much they enhanced the survival of the group – the fastest runner, the best man with a spear, the best man with a bow, the best fisher, the best Clovis point maker, the best healer, the best leader of the hunt, etc. No single alpha dude, but men who were held in differing levels of regard because of their innate and acquired skills. Accordingly, the greater the survival-enhancing skill set, the greater the status.

If anything had been a good predictor of a male's capacity to provide, protect, and garner community support for his mate and children, I'd put my money on his relative status. How would Lucy have clued into that? What fitness indicators could she rely on? The way people talked about a man for one, but I believe the way he carried himself, especially among his peers, and the way others treated him were the key signs.

A reasonable degree of status enables a man to be confident and relaxed among his peers, as he would have enjoyed greater regard and lesser aggression from other males. Even to this day, the higher the status a man has, the less likely he is to be a perpetrator or victim of aggression. Conversely, the greatest level of aggressive behaviour is found in those with the lowest status.

Relationship Tip: Why do otherwise great women sometimes select "bad boys" and other losers? Because they are biologically hardwired to detect what used to be positive fitness indicators (a guy with 'don't give a dang' attitude and who other men don't mess with). Unfortunately, those indicators are no longer valid in today's world; in fact, they're displayed most obviously by some of society's bottom feeders. The problem is, biologically based attractions are hard to control. What's a girl to do should she find herself attracted to a bad boy? Acknowledge the attraction, frame it as a false positive, and move on. Remember, there are evolved men out there who are high status, tough as nails when they have to be, yet compassionate, and emotionally intelligent. Save yourself – choose wisely.

Summarizing then, when an ancestral woman needed a mate to provide and protect, she was biologically bound to seek one who could best do that. In other words, it was a matter of survival to select a mate based on what he could do for her. After the emergence of civilizations, most women in most cultures were institutionally compelled to continue this strategy; trades, careers, even property ownership were often not an option for women in many cultures, and finding a husband was the only real avenue for material security. It is in this atmosphere that the institution of traditional marriage as we know it was born, and the legacy lives on.

Sociobiology and Today's Mating Game:

How does this relate to women today? I believe women remain hard-wired to seek mates and relationships that can provide them with a sense of security. Some selection is made consciously, as when favouring a guy with a good career. Some, however, remain unconscious because we all continue to respond to ancient fitness indicators, some of which are invalid today. Aside from the danger of being drawn to a bad choice as described above, the greatest danger of this to women is much more subtle.

Women in the Western world no longer "need" a mate to protect and provide as they once did, and if they favour that factor too heavily, they risk compromising their integrity and happiness. Worse still, if they opt for the old strategy of finding a guy to take care of them, they will severely hinder their personal development and long-term life satisfaction.

To help put this in perspective, men apparently have a corresponding biological drive that optimizes the continuation of their genes – impregnate (or at least try to) as many young females as they possibly can in their lifetimes. An extraordinary example of this is Genghis Khan, whose horrific habit of raping the women of the lands he conquered, is estimated to have given rise to 16 million direct male descendants today and roughly 0.5% of the world's population.[12]

Luckily, biology isn't destiny, and just because we have an instinctive desire, doesn't mean it's in our best interest to follow it. Men have new choices today, as do women. Women have the ability to embrace their own life path and acquire financial autonomy. They can do that and co-create a financially and emotionally interdependent relationship with a like-minded and -resourced mate.

So who did Lucy from our scenario above end up picking? The cute guy from the neighbouring tribe who was a really good dancer of course.

Feminine Essence and the Sacred Imperative

Another way to look at gender differences in the game of love is to consider it from a metaphysical stance. *Metaphysics* is a branch of philosophy that attempts to understand the basic nature of reality. Being less constrained than science, it can cross over into the realm of spirituality and other unobservable aspects of the universe. I believe what metaphysics has to say about human gender differences and mating is grounded in the biological and sociological forces acting on us. Despite the overlap, however, the voice and perspective of the meta-physician can cast an interesting

12. www.kuro5hin.org/story/2003/2/8/214236/6651

light on the issue.

One such metaphysical perspective addresses the differences between feminine and masculine energy or essence. A popular example of this can be found in the work of David Deida, whose book *Intimate Communion*,[13] I've drawn partially on here and recommend for reading. Earlier examples of this perspective can be found in such texts as Bubba Free John's *Love And The Two Armed Form*,[14] and from ancient philosophical perspectives such as the Taoist concept of yin-yang.

The notion of masculine and feminine essence is a compelling one; it's an elegant way to contemplate many of the core tendencies of men and women across time and culture. To boot, it's not even sexist: we are referring to energies, to two clusters of strong proclivities, and if we assume that females and males have both types that they can draw on, it becomes less a matter of gender and more a matter of one's preferred way of being. It just so happens that most women appear dominated by feminine essence and most men by masculine essence.

In general, the feminine is embodied by the very forces of nature. It is about creation, life, and change. The feminine is seen in the outrageous show of beauty that nature can put on, such as flowers, bird plumage (male and female), and autumn colours. Perhaps most importantly, the feminine is about interrelationship, the mutual interdependence that binds all forms of life together.

Embodied within the human form, whether in a male or female, the feminine seeks to create life and beauty, yearns for love and connection, and strives to nurture who and

13. David Deida (1995). Intimate Communion: Awakening Your Sexual Essence. Health Health Communications, Deerfield Beach, FL.
14. Free John, Bubba (1978) Love and the Two-armed Form. The Johannine Daist Communion.

what is loved. The feminine is ruled by the heart – the ever-moving dance of emotions, and its primary focus is on relationship.

So, if you are a female with a dominant feminine essence, what does that mean about your deepest desires and what will bring happy fulfillment in a relationship?

Love Rules:

The feminine will be most happy when all is well in one's relationship. When love and connection are solid, then the feminine is happy to the core. The things of the world, such as careers and finances take second place, and a committed union is often seen as a means to fulfilling its greatest imperative – to love fully and completely, and to create an emotional garden of fulfillment to share with her beloved. I believe this core desire generates much of the feminine resistance to the OYM, as embodied in the question...

"How can I build an enduring garden and put my life and love into it if I only have a one-year lease on the property?"

I'll provide the answer to that near the end of the chapter, but for now, I leave it as something to ponder.

Direction:

The feminine looks to the masculine for structure and direction. All women posses the masculine element and with it are quite capable of creating structure and goal-directed behaviour on their own. In a relationship, however, there is a strong preference to rely on their masculine-dominated partners for this grounding, directing force.

One of the traits that women most frequently identify as desirable in a mate is a man's ambition and his drive to fulfill it. The man who has a clear vision of his future and will not be swayed from it by acts of gods or men, will likely enjoy a powerful attraction by most women. This is the desire of the feminine to have a strong masculine force to balance it out.

Appreciation:

The feminine basks in attention and flourishes when surrounded by it. The multi-billion dollar fashion and cosmetic industries are a testament to that. Like a garden that no one visits, nothing is worse to the feminine than to put out the most beautiful display she can, and for it to go unnoticed or unappreciated.

The feminine will seek an observant and appreciative partner who will notice the beauty she has created (in self, home, and otherwise) and the nurturance she provides. The antithesis of this is a partner who does not notice or appreciate her and her gifts. The best marital arrangement then would be one that prevents her partner from taking her for granted.

Passion:

Let's not forget sex and passion. The excitement of sexual union comes largely from sexual polarity, when feminine and masculine energies come together with electric results. As with positive and negative electrical charges, the greater the difference between the two, the greater the spark. Translation, the more ruled you are by feminine essence, the more ruled by masculine essence your ideal (most electric) partner will need to be.

It is important to note that strong masculine essence does not translate to sexist pig. Deida writes of stages of development within the genders (see Deida, 1995). At stage one, men were men and women...well the little ladies were just fine staying home and taking care of the kids. Yes, that is sexist and is captured well by the 1940s and 1950s standard of the workingman and housewife. That was an era when these natural inclinations of most men and women were codified restraints on both genders. Doubt that men were losers in this as well? Can you imagine the ridicule a man in the 1950s would have faced if he stayed home and looked after the kids while his professional wife went out and brought home the bacon?

At stage two, which really took off in the 1960s and 1970s, all of the codified standards for men and women were challenged as sexist and there was a strong tendency to assume that men and women were essentially the same, anatomy aside. The essence of a couple in a stage two union: "Hey, honey, who's turn it is to change the oil in the truck?"

Having lived and done relationships through that era, and in that way, it was no surprise to me that women began singing songs about missing cowboys, and men secretly complained about the dearth of real women. Such is the fate of men and women with natural polarity trying to do relationships as though there were none, all in the name of political correctness.

Enter stage three, and I think you're going to love this. Imagine being in a relationship that embodied complete personal, political, and economic equality, and yet you and your partner were able to embrace your natural feminine and masculine essences and enjoy the electrical excitement that polarity brings. Imagine being "taken" (with your eager permission of course) by an uber-masculine partner who loved you deeply and saw you as his equal in every way? Now that's amore.

It is possible to have the best of both worlds: mind-blowing sexual polarity, and egalitarian equality, but only between two people living an evolved union. The problem as I see it is, contemporary marriage does not promote either very well.

What Women Say They Want

So that is what two hypothetical perspectives have to say on the matter, socio-biological and metaphysical, but what do women in the developed world actually say they want in their partners and from marriage? There is a lot of variation between women in this and the only desires that are important here are your own. There are exercises in the Appendix through which you can explore your ideal partner and relationship, but I've included a few commonly identified wishes below.

I've selected the following wish-list according to my personal and clinical investigations, and from perusing the results of surveys. Surveys are notoriously unreliable and can be quite biased, depending on how they are constructed and administered. Nevertheless, I've ventured to include the following because they are widely held and will be useful in contrasting the ability of conventional versus one-year marriages as vehicles of fulfillment.

To be loved, told so, and shown so regularly. This is something that men and women share as a top priority, though men are often more satisfied by being shown their partner's love rather than by being told. Consistent with the feminine imperative, love rules, and if it is missing or goes un-affirmed, even for a short time, a relationship can feel stagnant or barren.

Good communication. An essential skill and practice for any relationship that hopes to flourish, good communication is a desired trait in a mate and marriage. This includes the ability of one's partner to listen accurately, acknowledge and respect her thoughts and feelings, and express his own thoughts and feelings in a mature and respectful way. It also includes a partner's ability and willingness to listen to her trials and tribulations without trying to fix things.

The willingness to take time for her and the relationship. Women want to know they are important and want their partners to show it by taking the time for them. It is important that a woman's partner prioritize time for doing life together. Romance is always a relished ingredient in this, and there are a lot more options than poetry and flowers.

Emotional and financial stability in a partner and security in the relationship. Although this has changed somewhat as women have become empowered to make their own way in the world without the assistance of a man, having a partner who is financially and emotionally solvent remains high on the priorities list, as does the prospect of a secure and stable relationship. Without these, life might prove to be a struggle and the relationship conflict-ridden.

A man with *confidence and self-respect, who takes care of himself physically and emotionally, is independent, and who does not exhibit clingy behaviour*. This desired set of traits is a perennial favourite and probably hasn't changed much in historic times. Along with the traits of *ambition, industriousness, education, and intelligence*, these are the hallmarks of a man with direction and focus, the proverbial "good provider."

Respect for her space and privacy. This sounds like the sort of thing men have always desired – several degrees of freedom within a relationship. I'm not so certain that this represents a shift in feminine consciousness as much as it reflects the realities of today – women have lives outside of their relationships and want space and privacy that men have historically fought for and enjoyed.

A happy and stable union for raising children. No need to comment much on this one. It is only common sense that, male or female, one would want to provide a happy and stable environment for one's children. This will be discussed in detail in chapter five.

Finally, for many women, marriage appears to serve as a form of validation of self and relationship, a public declaration that she is important enough to her partner (and vice versa) that he took *a vow of commitment* to her.

In addition to the above, there is the usual cluster of desired knightly traits, such as honesty, integrity, loyalty, chivalry, dependability, and a willingness and ability to protect. There is a cluster of desired traits that promise pleasantries when around her partner, such as a sense of humour, fair sharing of workload, good manners, good hygiene, sociability, and that he is good at being a friend.

So if the above are some of the common desires women report having for their men and their relationships, how well does contemporary marriage help them turn the desire into a reality? Well, if statistics, social surveys, and clinical experience mean anything, the answer is middling to poor.

How Traditional Marriage Fails Women

Not long ago, I heard a radio report on a new study that found married men in their forties and fifties to be healthier and happier than their single peers, and the opposite to be true of women – single women in their forties and fifties were found to be healthier and happier than their married counterparts. Intrigued, I researched the matter of who seemed to benefit more from marriage – men or women. It didn't surprise me to find reports weighing in on both sides of the equation and many sitting in the middle.

What I became more aware of during this research was just how controversial the issue is, and I tend to assume that, as with war, the first casualty of controversy is truth. My final cautious conclusions? Marriage can provide wonderful benefits for both men and women: it can be a major source of joy and satisfaction for both; it can be a major source of stress and disappointment for both; and a bad marriage appears to impact the mental and physical health of women more so than men. Women, on average, do appear to bear a disproportionate amount of the workload on the business side of marriage and they are the ones who initiate divorce roughly 70% to 90% of the time.[15]

Setting the numbers and controversy aside, I don't see much point in debating whether marriage is beneficial or detrimental, or whether it favours one gender over the other. Marriage, in one form or another, is here to stay and a more useful inquiry is what can be done to make marriage work better. To do that, we first need to identify common sources of dissatisfaction within it.

To that end, I've compiled a brief list of the most common reasons I've heard expressed by women for their dissatisfaction in their marriages and with their partners. These include:

- I no longer feel loved and appreciated;
- He doesn't listen to me;
- I have a full-time job too, but he doesn't do his fair share of work around the house;
- He works too much and neglects me / the family;
- I feel controlled – it's okay for him to get out and enjoy his friends but when I want my girl's night out, he gives me a hard time;
- He has not taken care of himself physically;
- He drinks too much;
- He watches too much TV;
- He's financially irresponsible and we can never get on top of the bills;

---

15. http://en.wikipedia.org/wiki/Divorce

- He's become so dependent on me to do so much for him, I sometimes feel like his mother;

- Between work, the kids, and my husband, I feel too many people are demanding too much from me;

- I do for others but I rarely do for myself;

- I feel so lost I no longer know what I want for myself;

When I look at that list, and the many others I've read in clinical reports and surveys, it strikes me that the causes of marital dissatisfaction for many women distil down to two issues: 1. They are not getting what they desire from their partners; and 2. They have lost their way in their personal journey through life. I believe both are consequences of what we often hope for from a marital union, and of the conditions and expectations commonly established by traditional marriage. Below are three core expectations that I believe set the stage for personal and marital decline, and which the mythology around marriage perpetuates.

My soul-mate will complete me. We all have growing edges, areas of our personal development that are weak or lacking. When you approach a relationship as a means to complete yourself or compensate for those edges, you rob yourself of the drive and opportunity to grow. As a consequence, you hinder your personal development. At the same time, you'll place the heavy strain of unrealizable expectations on the bond with your partner, a strain that is likely to sabotage the very thing you desire most.

It is one thing to enjoy a degree of interdependence in a marriage in which you both "lean on" the strengths of the other, sometimes specializing to a degree in the tasks of running the business side of things. This is where the differing strengths of the masculine and feminine essences can really compliment each other. It is another thing, however, to allow one's self to become dependent on a partner for something you ought to be able to do for yourself.

If I marry a partner with a good career, I'll not have to worry so much about my own. This is based on the old notion that a woman can obtain financial security by marrying the right guy, one with good resources. At a minimum, it can detract from your focus on your own career and resources; at its worst, it can lead to financial dependency and a loss of sovereignty. With those come decreased self-esteem and life satisfaction.

Marriage brings security. This is the notion that you can obtain emotional security through marriage. In actuality, true security can only come from within, and men or women looking for relationship-based security eventually discover it to be an illusion. It is true that being in a committed, loving relationship is a great catalyst that helps generate a feeling of security, that feeling is nevertheless generated from within, from the true source of all well-being. Looking to another or to a relationship to provide this can prevent you from tapping into that deep and dependable well.

These three expectations are mythically tied to marriage, and if not guarded against, they can collectively impede your personal growth and compromise your sovereignty. They can also lead both men and women into the pitfall of partner manipulation and control.

When our sense of completeness, direction, and financial/emotional security are hitched to our partner, it creates a compelling need to ensure that person will be there for us. Such emotional dependency almost always leads to hypervigilance for threats to the relationship and efforts to control that person. A logical description would sound like this – "If I depend on someone for something important to me, then to feel like I'm in control of my life (a fundamental psychological need) I need to have a way of ensuring I get what I need – I need to have control over that person."

This can take the form of spying and stalking, criticism and complaints, and outright dictating and forbidding. These are incredibly toxic behaviours and are always damaging for both partners. Ironically, if a woman so inclined does manage to control her partner, she's likely to lose interest in him as a lover – a man who can be controlled is not a man with an unwavering drive – one of the core fitness indicators the feminine is drawn to. Any way you look at it, it's a lose-lose situation.

In summary, between the general negative effects discussed in chapter one and those discussed above, I believe traditional marriage doesn't serve women well in today's social and economic realities. Perhaps it did when women did not have the career and lifestyle options they enjoy today, and perhaps it still serves them well in the parts of the undeveloped world. In the past it was legal protection for when a woman agreed to marry a man and become economically dependent on him. Today, that benefit has become a liability as it encourages a loss of sovereignty and can help set a trap that is difficult to escape. There is a better way.

The One Year Marriage: A Woman's BFF?

In my experience discussing the OYM with patients, colleagues, and friends over the years, a common reaction is that it is an arrangement that would benefit men more than women. I believe just the opposite is true, that women have more to gain from it.

Structural Support

The structural aspect of the One Year Marriage reflects the masculine: it's about taking care of business first, setting rules and boundaries and aiming for a sense of fairness.

Paradoxically, it is by using the structure of an agreement to create clean rules of engagement and disengagement (the masculine) that the space and conditions are set that will enable the emotional side of the relationship to flourish (the feminine). In other words, honouring the masculine by way of the OYM results in honouring the feminine by way of a thriving bond of love.

Retained Sovereignty

In the 1995 movie version of *The Little Princess*,[16] the tale begins with a young girl being told by her nanny, "All women are princesses – it is our right." That is a beautiful assertion, so why not embrace it as truth. All women are princesses and all men are princes. What a nice way to look at the world about us.

We would all be wiser and happier in my opinion if we chose to view our selves and everyone around us as royalty. Imagine what the world might come to if we treated each other with that sort of respect. Well the happy news is that you can choose to do just that. Consider yourself a princess or, if you're a mother, a queen. How are you to retain your sovereign rights and identity when the right prince or king comes along?

One of the best ways to do that is to mind your own business, so to speak, and retain your lands and titles (i.e., your property, career, and control of your finances). In a OYM you're encouraged, if not compelled, to do just that. This can prevent you from becoming financially dependent on a partner, something that still sadly happens today. Women who want to rely on their partners for financial security pay a huge price for this: they lose their independence and a large share of their self-respect, and they degrade the quality of the great love they deeply want.

---

16. The Little Princess (1995). Warner Brothers Pictures

Reduced Economic Vulnerability

This is a natural outcome of retained sovereignty, but it is worth separate mention. We make ourselves vulnerable in matters of love. We open our hearts and step forward, loving and wanting to be loved in return. In this, we put our souls on the line, we risk our hearts. Perhaps this is how it should be – must be – to acquire one of the greatest gifts life has to offer. However, there is no reason, no nobility or benefit, to making ourselves vulnerable in other ways. Our hearts are a sufficient offering for love; our material resources do not have to be a part of that.

A Good Defence Against Abuse

Guess what – spousal abuse is alive and well. It comes in several broad forms (physical, emotional, financial, and sexual) but the core pattern is the same – your partner takes you for granted and has cultivated moderate to high levels of emotional and financial dependency in you, you've become socially isolated, and you're being mistreated. He or she is in control and there is not much you dare to do about it.

A key benefit of the OYM is that neither partner will be particularly vulnerable to this sort of control or abuse. To control or abuse someone, you must first gain power over that person. When I talk about control, I'm not talking about stepping up and taking charge of a situation or assuming delightful control in moments of making love. I'm referring to one person's ability to exert wilful control over another's life, for an extended period, against that person's preferences. I'm referring to someone pressuring a partner to not work, to dump his or her friends, to not wear attractive clothing, to give up a hobby, etc.

Similarly, when I talk about abuse, I'm not talking about a simple financial, emotional, or physical assault because that can happen to almost anyone (and in saying that I am by no means condoning it). I'm referring to someone exploiting another financially, repeatedly assaulting that person's self-esteem, and/or repeatedly hurting her/him physically.

Both control and abuse are more common than you think because most of the time it is subtle and can go on for years before its effects become obvious. One certain way to prevent both, however, is for you to maintain a sense of dignity, integrity, and both emotional and financial sovereignty. It would be much more difficult for you to lose your sovereignty in a OYM than in a traditional union.

Another way that negotiating a OYM can help protect a woman from abuse is the fact that the majority of abusers are emotionally immature and insecure. Such individuals would be unlikely to agree to a OYM in the first place – when one's partner has retained her or his emotional and financial ability to leave a relationship, and do so without penalty, it might well feel too risky to abuse that person in any way. Abusers prey on dependent individuals and on the tendency of such people to recoil when hurt but choose not to leave.

Constructive Insecurity

One of the things that makes love sweet in its infancy is its tentative nature; being uncertain of the other person's willingness to accept us as we are during the dance of intimacy. Because we are rarely certain about what a new beau thinks or feels about us, we are challenged to be aware of our selves and how we are impacting each other. In this, new relationships can promote self-awareness and growth, and encourage us to be more attentive to the connection in a healthy way. This fosters intimacy and trust, which are two elements that one might hope for in a long-term committed relationship, but which all too often diminish under the illusion of security that a traditional marriage fosters.

Similarly, the built-in impermanence of a OYM can, as discussed in chapter two, engender a sense of *constructive insecurity* that promotes attending to the needs of the self, one's partner, and the quality of the union. Things are often not well appreciated until we are at risk of losing them. In developing relationships, as soon as things feel "secure," people often shift their priorities to other challenges. I believe men, in their sacred quest for the ultimate mission (see chapter four), tend to do this more than women, but both genders are prone to it. The key, then, is to cultivate an ongoing awareness that your partner has the freedom and the emotional and financial capacity to leave the union if things go south. The result: both partners will be encouraged to be more attentive.

Enduring Desire

An important way that a OYM can benefit women is that it can help preserve one of the most cherished aspects of a relationship – sexual excitement. As mentioned earlier, sexual electricity tends to be felt in proportion to sexual polarity between two people. Maintaining the level of sexual excitement we often experience with a new partner over the long haul is largely a matter of maintaining sexual polarity and openness to love.

To do that, both partners have to allow and be allowed the freedom to be true to who and what they are. To even use the term "allow" implies that somehow we have the authority over our partners to allow or disallow their behaviour. Are you a parent or a lover? If you think in terms of "allowing" something in your union, then honey, you're missing the boat.

Most women; due to their dominant feminine essence, tend to yearn for a strong, masculine male who is his own man, someone with a clear mission in life who cannot be diverted from it by acts of men or gods. What do you imagine would happen to your feelings toward this rare male should you be able to 'control' him? Short answer = depolarization = loss of sexual / romantic interest. His interest in you will deflate as well and he will either leave, if he is still man enough, or he will physically stay but leave emotionally. That describes the state of a lot of traditional marriages I have encountered in my work.

To try to gain control over your male partner is to invest in the death of the relationship and the best way to avoid trying to control him is to eliminate the primary motivation for doing so – fear. Fear and the controlling behaviour it generates in relationships is a product of insecurity and its twin sibling, dependency. Whether it's financial or emotional in nature, the result is the same. The greater the dependency and insecurity, the greater the felt need for control. It's as simple as that.

The complement of this also holds true: allowing your male partner to control you sabotages the relationship as well. Not only will it undermine your self-esteem and happiness, it will result in a loss of interest in you as well. Some men have a strong desire to control their partners (see hint below); however, men sometimes acquire control when they don't even want it, as when their partners are too passive or compliant. When that happens, interest in her usually fades.

> *Relationship Tip: Some men, out of their own insecurity, have a strong need to control their partners. As a rule of thumb, the greater the insecurity, the greater the need for control, and yes my dear, that uber-masculine bad boy may well be the town's biggest wuss beneath the tough veneer. Any sign that your partner is controlling should be viewed as a yellow flag and addressed immediately and assertively. If it continues or recurs repeatedly, it is best considered a deal-breaker.*

The best way to tame or eliminate this toxic dependency and insecurity in your life is to retain your sovereignty and independence. I know of no better way to do that than to approach a romantic union as though it were a time-limited gift to embrace and enjoy, something that could be renewed if the love between you and your partner remains strong. In other words, a One Year Marriage.

Romantic Commitment

It may not seem intuitively right to claim that the OYM engenders a greater amount of romantic commitment, but think about it – is romance not a courageous act of the heart? If you think about the great romantic tales of book and screen, are the two lovers not at the edge of some disaster or dissolution most of the time?

Committing to another when you have the legal protection of a traditional marriage and the economic and social bondage that goes with that certainly takes a degree of courage and faith, but not nearly so much as when there is no safety net other than what you provide for yourself. The OYM demands courage, awareness, self-sufficiency, and joyous interdependence like no other arrangement.

I posed a similar questions in an earlier chapter: which seems more romantic – two people journeying through life together, bound by love, dependence, and legal and economic obligations; or two people journeying through life together, bound by love, interdependence, and the simple choice to be together? Which takes more courage of heart? Which would promote greater personal growth and self-responsibility?

The OYM is deeply romantic. It is placing your heart and soul on the line when nothing but your mutual desire to be with each other binds the two of you together.

Deep, Mature Love

Another benefit of the OYM is in finding the sort of love most of us long for. The only true way to find a love that is as deeply fulfilling as we often dream of, is to evolve to sufficient completeness that we lose the "need" for another. When we have adequate love and respect for ourselves, knowing we can stand alone, only then can we enjoy a bond that is based on a true appreciation for our partners and ourselves.

Now that women do have the option of careers and can create a good life for themselves without depending on a partner, their true liberation is at hand and the means to an evolved life does not depend on finding a mate. Sadly, many still feel the remnants of biological and societal bondage and still hold a man's ability 'to provide' as a prime consideration when seeking a mate.

If instead of looking for a mate to provide for her, a woman were to commit to her personal evolution and seek a like-minded partner equally committed to his, would she not optimize her potential for a truly fulfilling life? Would she not be more likely to find a deep love and soul mate?

So to answer that earlier question: *how can you build an enduring garden and put your life and love into it if you only have a one-year lease on the property?* By embracing impermanence – by making it an act of mindful devotion, internalizing what is most important about it so it is yours forever, and letting go of the rest.

By remaining present and accepting something for what it is, right now, and detaching from any fantasy that it must or will continue on indefinitely, you open your mind and heart to the true gifts your garden has to offer. Then if winter or a storm comes and the garden does not return in the spring, you will have lost nothing.

Chapter 4

The Masculine Perspective

"Those who talk most about the blessings of marriage and the constancy of its vows are the very people who declare that if the chain were broken and the prisoners left free to choose, the whole social fabric would fly asunder. You cannot have the argument both ways. If the prisoner is happy, why lock him in? If he is not, why pretend that he is?" ~ *George Bernard Shaw*

What are Men Looking for From Marriage?

So what do men really want in a relationship, desire from love and marriage? The stereotypes would have us believe that we're simple creatures who only want a young, beautiful woman to cater to our whims; give us amazing sex anytime, anyplace; and to keep it simple and uncomplicated on the emotional side. Perhaps there's a degree of truth to that, but research and my own personal and clinical experiences have taught me that what we really want is a lot more complicated. In fact, what we want from a romantic union is not that different from what women want; after all, men and women are both human and are far more alike than different.

As in chapter three, I'll approach this from several levels, starting from the broad lens of sociobiology, shifting to the metaphysical level of gender essence, and finally to reporting on some of the common things men say they want from a union with their partners.

Sociobiology 101

As described in chapter three, sociobiology strives to explain the social behaviour of animals in terms of their adaptive, evolutionary significance. Its close cousin, evolutionary psychology,[17] tends to zero in on the same essential traits that would maximize a male's mating success, defined as how well his genetic code passed forward to future generations.

Some of the speculations below are my own and may not bear up under rigid scientific scrutiny; however, that's not important – it's not meant to represent the cutting edge in the field. Rather, it is offered as an example of how sociobiology might explain some well-documented and near-universal human male tendencies in the mating game.

It's a reasonable and common assumption that selective pressures in the early years of our species would have favoured men who successfully pursued women who were the most fertile and capable of caring for their children for at least 10 years. Given the limited life span and the risks of childbirth back then, this likely meant that healthy young women with no other children to care for were the prime females to seek.

We can see a product of this selective pressure to this day in the fact that males, as a rule, are most physically attracted to young females with strong healthy bodies.[18] Women today know this instinctively, as the multi-billion dollar youth enhancing, age-defying industry will bear witness. Keep in mind I'm talking only about physical attraction here; other factors play key roles today in who men select for their mates.

---

17. http://en.wikipedia.org/wiki/Evolutionary_psychology
18. See Buss (1994). The Evolution of Desire: Strategies of Human Mating. Harper Collins, New York.

One of the central issues to consider when speculating about what selective pressures our ancient ancestors faced is the amount of "parental investment" they were compelled to make; in other words, how much time, energy, and resources were required to successfully pass one's DNA on to the next generation.

For females, it is universally substantial to the extreme, whereas for males, it can range from near nothing at all to substantial. Accordingly, the parental investment of males is usually considered to be moderate on average; however, it's important to note the possible range in investment, as it is my belief that this gave rise to two divergent mating strategies for our male ancestors.

One strategy would have been to impregnate as many females as possible in one's lifetime (i.e., a quantity strategy). Think about this: if Player Pete impregnated 200 women (he tends to visit other bands a lot) and provided them with nothing other than a pleasant evening, while Decent Dan mated with one special female and provided for and protected her and their few children, who would likely leave the most genetic code for the generations to come?

The proposal of a 'quantity strategy' stems from simple considerations of gene expression as in Dawkins' Selfish Gene Hypothesis.[19] Perhaps it is the basis of the male tendency to be less selective than females when deciding with whom they are willing to have sex, and to have a wandering eye. Perhaps it can explain why psychopaths walk among us (see *James Bond...* below), but I believe social factors likely imposed counteracting selective pressures on our ancient ancestors.

What we know about hunter-gatherer groups in historic times suggests that not much could have gone on in the

---

19. Dawkins, R (1976) The Selfish Gene. Oxford University Press, London.

small tribal groups of our ancient ancestors without everyone knowing about it. Women have mates, fathers, and brothers and I think it safe to suggest that men in those days had at least as strong a tendency to be protective of their female kin as they do today. Unless Player Pete was very careful in his amorous pursuits, he'd likely be killed or cast out for bad behaviour.

I suspect that the male polyamorous tendency and the social chaos it could produce if not checked was the basis for our earliest sexual prohibitions and mating rituals (i.e., some form a socially sanctioned marriage). I imagine that the quantity mating strategy of Player Pete was likely checked by social factors that favoured the second mating strategy – to mate with one or only a few females in a lifetime and to provide for and defend (a quality strategy).

Perhaps most men today possess a residual inclination to assume a quantity strategy, but I believe cultural pressures have caused us to evolve beyond that. I believe we also have traits that encourage if not compel us to find one special female and bond deeply with her and our resulting children – the quality strategy. One of the dangers to men of using a quality strategy, however, is that it results in selective pressures similar to that which females faced – it would have been critical that our few offspring survived to have their own children.

So then what traits might have optimized mating success using a quality strategy? You can do the exercise yourself and come up with your own list, but mine includes:

- An attraction to young and healthy females;
- An attraction to females who exhibit a giving, kind, and nurturing nature (she will be the primary caregiver of your offspring and if she helped keep you healthy and happy as well, bonus);

- An attraction to other traits that would encourage him to stick around and help out (e.g., playfulness, a high libido);
- An aversion to traits in women that might reduce her mothering capacity or his willingness to spend time with her (e.g., selfishness, aggressiveness).

Now take this into consideration – one of the worst things that can happen to a male, biologically speaking, is to find himself providing for and protecting another man's offspring. Unless the other male is one's identical twin brother, being cuckolded is a genetic disaster, second only to not leaving any offspring of your own at all. In the Western world today, it's not so much an issue because a man can usually help raise another man's children without detracting from the health and wellness of his own. However, back in the day, when you were probably lucky to successfully raise two or three children who would then go on to breed, it would have been a genetic catastrophe.

Women always know who their children are, but men can rarely know with complete certainty (unless of course you can lock her in a tower and hang on to the key). Women are known to have wandering eyes as well and there is evidence that one variant female mating strategy is to have one male to provide for her, and to become impregnated by one or more other males. For example, when women have sex with partners outside of their pair bonds, they tend to do so around the time of ovulation,[20] as though part of an innate strategy to successfully have another male's children. Various genetic studies have estimated that a percentage of births wherein the identified father had not actually sired the child to be as low as 4% and as high as 25%.[21] Are you concerned

20. E.g., Gangestad, S. W., Thornhill, R., & Garver, C. E. (2002). Changes in women's sexual interests and their partners' mate retention tactics across the menstrual cycle: Evidence for shifting conflicts of interest. Proceedings of the Royal Society of London B, 269, 975_982.

yet, gentlemen?

Going back to Lucy's band 70,000 years ago, if we assume there were at least a few Player Petes around, and that even Decent Dan might accept a wayward female's invitation for a quickie by the river, what traits would a male opting for a quality strategy have had to exhibit to optimize his mating success? How about:

- A strong tendency to minimize access to his mate by other men;
- A strong tendency to be watchful of his mate for signs of a wandering eye;
- An attraction to females who exhibited a demure and chaste character;
- An attraction to females who appear to bond tightly to their mates;
- An aversion to females who were sexually aggressive.

Today, we refer to those traits as being jealous, controlling, and sexist, but back in the day, they may have been critical to our biological success, at least for those opting for the quality strategy.

This all sounds very clinical and devoid of emotion so lets turn to matters of the heart. Above all else, I believe the trait that would have optimized mating success for our early male and female forbears would have been the capacity to form strong emotional bonds – love. Love, in its many forms, and the resulting desire to care for and protect the objects of our affections, would have motivated a lot of behaviours that would have resulted in increased survival of family members and hence genetic, biological success.

James Bond – good, bad, or ugly? The majority of young

---

21. E.g., The REPORT Newsmagazine 2000-04-24: "The rate of wrongful paternity in 'stable monogamous marriages,' according to the Max Planck Institute in Munich, Germany, ranges from one in 10 with the first child to one in four with the fourth".

men and more than a few older men appear to romanticize the quantity mating strategy. What Western male hasn't thought of James Bond as a heroic role model – a man to be reckoned with who jets about the world, enjoying the company of a half-dozen beautiful women in every movie.

For most, this icon remains a fantasy, an outlet for the primal desire to mate with many females, and for those who do play the field with enthusiasm, it may amount to a win-win recreational ideal. However, for those who actually aspire to the icon or who are not mindful of how they affect the objects of their amorous pursuits, ponder this...

To be successful at a quantity strategy, an ancestral male would have had to possess an effective blend of certain qualities. These include: persuasiveness and a degree of superficial charm; a reduced capacity to feel remorse; a reduced ability to emotionally bond with others; a willingness to transgress social mores; and a willingness to betray the trust of those close to him. In psychology, we used to call those folks psychopaths. We call them other things these days but the new terms don't quite capture their character like 'psychopath'.

So yes, some of the traits of the quintessential male hero, James Bond, are those of a psychopath, and if you truly aspire to such yourself, you're aiming for membership in a club of social parasites.

Sociobiology and Today's Mating Game

What does all this mean for a boy who's out to find the girl of his dreams today? As asserted in chapter three, biology is not destiny, but it has left us with instinctive attractions, drives, and other tendencies that have to be reckoned with in today's mating game.

One such tendency is being guarded about our partner's access to other men and vice versa. Left unbridled in today's world, we call that jealous, controlling behaviour and it is extraordinarily toxic. If it's not a deal-breaker for your prospective partner, it will corrode any relationship the two of you develop and neither of you will be truly happy. The good news is that locking one's mate away in a proverbial tower is no longer a biological necessity today – being cuckolded is one-hundred-percent preventable.

If a male ever doubts the paternity of his children, or even if he is simply curious, genetic testing is fast, inexpensive, and extremely reliable. Besides, helping raise another man's children is becoming more the norm than the exception by way of blended families. As long as a man knows for certain that he is the biological father of some of the children he is helping raise, his biological imperative to procreate is satisfied.

> **Relationship Tip:** *Although jealousy may be a natural reaction to the threat of losing a mate to another, it is an emotion we are better off without, as it no longer serves a useful purpose. What can you do if you tend to be jealous? That's a whole other book – here's the short version.*
>
> *If jealousy is uncharacteristic of you, then explore why you're feeling jealous – you may learn something about yourself and/or your partner. It may be an intuitive signal that something is amiss in the relationship or with your partner's or your own commitment to the relationship. It may also signal that some latent insecurity in you has been activated and so dealing with it becomes a growth opportunity.*
>
> *If jealously is a common emotion for you, then I strongly suggest counselling or therapy to help you uncover the insecurity that is generating it. You will be happier and more grounded for it. In either case, the bottom line is this: your feelings of jealousy are your own and are not caused by your partner, nor is it his or her responsibility to fix or prevent them.*

Another benefit to recognizing our socio-biological heirlooms is that it gives us more leeway in what character traits are viable in a mate. On the one hand, traits such as sexual aggressiveness in women can trigger an innate negative reaction in some men, but if such a woman was an otherwise great catch, those men could work through their archaic reaction and learn to enjoy it. On the other hand, some traits that may be naturally attractive, such as being demure and gentle, may not actually fit well with your desired lifestyle. In such cases, you can simply acknowledge the attraction for what it is and move on.

How about physical beauty? Most of us are attracted to it, but is it a good predictor of how good a mate or mother a woman will make, of how successful your children will be in passing on their genes? Does it even predict how happy you will be with her? Totally not! As a modern fitness indicator, beauty is irrelevant and can, like the lure of the anglerfish, entice you to be someone's lunch if possessed by the wrong person.

Don't get me wrong, I would never suggest that a disproportionate number of beautiful women are nasty characters or make lousy mates; I've know a fair few beautiful women who would make amazing mates, combining intelligence with compassion and a fun-loving nature. It's just that too many men appear willing to overlook characteristics that would otherwise make a woman a bad partner for them, simply because she's a looker.

If you doubt this, get into a frank discussion with a few twenty-something beauties and you'll hear all about how much of a sap most guys are, and how they (the women) can be assured a free night out at the bar by just showing up and allowing their pursuers to buy their way for them. That is just bad behaviour on their part, and suggests an entitlement issue or some other character flaw. In any case, such behaviour should garner serious points against them if you are seeking a good mate.

The bottom line – beauty can be a gift of nature to enjoy, but as a strong biological trigger, it can also be a lure into something you don't really want. Perhaps the best attitude toward it is this: "Beauty may catch my attention, but it won't hold it long – show me what you're really made of." If you sit back and imagine a prospective partner as though she were unattractive, is her behaviour still tolerable, do you still want to share time and space? There is another suggestion I make in the Appendix, which is this: "Choose your partner as though you were blind. How does she feel to be with?"

Awareness is the key. Being aware of what attracts us in a woman and why, gives us the power to choose whether to heed that attraction or exercise "rational resistance to an unwise urge" as the song goes.[22]

I could go on for several chapters about the sociobiology of the mating game but my purpose has just been to give you a taste of plausible biological bases for some of the male tendencies in dating and mating. It's a fascinating field of speculation and I encourage you to continue it on your own, but the key benefit is simply to recognize that some of your inclinations and desires have a biological basis that may or may not serve you well. Like our proclivity to consume salty, fatty, and sweet foods; it may have helped us survive in prehistoric times, but it's a root cause of degenerative disease and premature death today.

Masculine Essence and the Sacred Imperative

A useful metaphysical perspective on the game of love is one that looks at masculine and feminine energies, two clusters of strong proclivities.[23] As discussed in chapter

22. Rush. *Prime Mover.*
23. See David Deida (1995). Intimate Communion: Awakening Your Sexual Essence.

three, the notion of masculine and feminine essence is a compelling and elegant way to think about many of the apparent differences between the genders. We assume that in most women the feminine dominates and in most men the masculine dominates.

Keep in mind that men and women are far more similar than they are different and that both genders possess both energy forms to draw on. Accordingly, women can excel at tasks usually considered masculine and vice versa, but it is a matter of one's preferred way of being.

These differences have been seen in similar ways across cultures and time. In general, the masculine is enamoured of linear progression, rational thought, purpose, and the freedom to engage a purpose. To the masculine, life is a quest.

So if you are a male, transgender, or some other variant of gender identity that is primarily ruled by masculine essence, what does this suggest about your deepest desires, what will make you fulfilled and happy in a relationship?

Support for Your Quest

Since the most important thing to the masculine is the quest (which may be as simple as fixing the lawnmower, or as grand as reversing global warming), your primary requirement for a happy relationship will be a partner who gets it. A partner who understands your need to immerse yourself in your mission and can give you the time and space to do so will endear you like few other qualities. If your partner also happens to believe in your quest and actively supports you in it, perhaps you've found a soul mate.

Degrees of Freedom

The masculine soul yearns for a worthy quest and

Health Communications, Deerfield Beach, FL.

languishes when one is not in clear focus. When clarity of purpose is lacking, the masculine needs the freedom to withdraw within, to "go to the mountain top" and commune with the powers to find it. When the masculine has its focus, it needs the freedom and ability to pursue it. Similarly, when the masculine feels overwhelmed by the demands of the quest, there is a strong need to escape and re-muster.

Much has been said about men's lust for freedom, their reluctance to marry at times, their incessant escapes from their partners (whether to the garage, fishing stream, or Afghanistan), but I believe it all comes down to this simple need for time and space to attain clarity and then pursue the quest. Find a partner who understands that and supports you in it, and you'll long for her embrace in the quiet moments of the quest.

> *Relationship Tip: Although it is an integral part of the masculine to find and pursue the quest, it is only half of the saga — the hero always comes home and marries the girl. Just as our muscles need rest and recuperation (in fact, after a heavy workout, the growth takes place during sleep), we need the balance of the garden to rest in, and the embrace of love. In fact, I believe the questing of the masculine is, at its heart, about clearing the space for a garden and attracting a desirable embodiment of the feminine. Learning to shift gears into relationship mode on a frequent basis, and relaxing into the feminine (be it from within or from your partner) is critical to the overall health and happiness of yourself and your relationship.*

Respect for Boundaries

The masculine tends to compartmentalize life into different areas of endeavour. Without this and with the whole questing going on (career and the ten quests involved there, fixing the darn lawn-mower again, finally hooking that huge bass that's been playing with you for months, yada,

yada) the masculine would be readily confused and overwhelmed.

One consequence of this is the masculine is enamoured of boundaries and the rules that support them. This masculine inclination in the evolved person, whether male or female, can give rise to fighting for human rights and justice. In the un-evolved person, it can give rise to rigid, moralistic rules that must be followed by everyone. In a relationship, it can foster fairness and healthy boundaries, or set the stage for a veritable chess game of control.

The masculine will be happiest with a partner who understands the importance of fair rules and healthy boundaries, who can work with the masculine to establish them, and then is willing to respect them. It is not about the masculine setting and enforcing the rules, but about the masculine and feminine coming together to co-create the set of ground guidelines that will serve them both. If the masculine is partnered with someone who cannot do this, he will be forever frustrated.

Respect for and Acceptance of the Masculine

This is all about essence polarity, the sacred dance between the masculine and feminine. Taking a look at the Taoist yin-yang symbol – two distinct figures, each a mirror complement of the other, make up the whole. One is no greater than the other and one cannot exist, as a whole, without the other. Such is the case with masculine and feminine energies. Equal and balanced, the forces of the masculine and feminine combine to make the whole and neither can exist without the other.

For a relationship to be whole, the partners must come together in mutual acceptance and respect. That means neither can have 'issues' with men or women; people with unresolved gender issues, cannot completely accept and embrace both masculine and feminine energies, and are not at peace with themselves. The result – they are not capable of coming together with another in a healthy, joyous union. This is true of same gender partnerships and relationships based on other gender identity variants.

As an illustrative aside, I've worked with quite a few hundred survivors of childhood sexual abuse and sexual assault and I've observed something both pervasive and sad. When a survivor's anger and mistrust has generalized from his or her perpetrator to all members of the perpetrator's gender, they typically have very strained if not hostile relationships with members of that gender. That may not be surprising or unexpected, but there is also a strong tendency to have problematic relationships with members of the other gender as well. When engaging in therapy, I usually find evidence of a deep internal split. It is as though the trauma of the abuse had fractured the survivor's psyche, severing the connection between his or her masculine and feminine aspects. Without being at peace within, they have an exceedingly difficult time being at peace with anyone. Good healing inevitably involves coming to be at peace with the offending gender and embracing its characteristics internally.

Both men and women will only reach their potential for fulfillment in this life if they are at peace with all aspects of the feminine and masculine, and they will only be happy with partners who are likewise at peace. I have stressed this here because in my clinical work I have seen more rejection of the masculine than the feminine in both men and women.

When men do not fully accept their own masculine traits, they emotionally and behaviourally castrate themselves. If they are partnered with such a person, their partner will forever attempt to do likewise. The bottom line: you'll be happiest with a partner who loves and fully accepts masculine energy and traits.

Passionate Polarity

This is very closely tied to the previous point but relates to one of men's favourite subjects – sex. Like complementary electrical poles, when the positive and negative come together you get sparks. When it refers to sex, you get fireworks. As with electricity, the greater the potential the greater the difference between the positive and negative charges the greater the spark.

If you are a man who's dominated by the masculine, you will experience the greatest sexual joy and connection if:

1. You are completely accepting of your masculine energy and traits;

2. You feel comfortable expressing your masculine energy toward the feminine (with your partner's eager permission of course);

3. Your partner is dominated by the feminine and is completely accepting of that;

4. Your partner is comfortable with opening to the energy of the masculine.

When a couple can come together under these circumstances, you do get the proverbial fireworks – transcendent sexual union.

Does this mean you're best off to hook up with a girly-girl? Not at all! You partner can be the CEO of a company, an Olympic calibre athlete, and she might even be able to kick your butt. Her essential core, however – the woman she is when the enemy has been repelled, the dinner is ready, and it's time to kick back for the evening – does need to be feminine and both willing and able to relax into that.

What Men Say They Want

What do men say they want from a marriage? Keep in mind that there is variation in what men want and that the only desires that are important here are your own; however, I've included a few commonly expressed wishes for discussion. The list isn't exhaustive and some points may not apply to you at all.

If you're interested you can take up the mission of doing a little Google research on the matter. You can also look ahead to the Appendix where you'll find explorations to help you clarify what you want, and what your ideals for a mate and relationship are.

A willing and loving partner who loves and wants us for who we are. Men want women who will still love and respect them when their faults and weaknesses surface, and who will stand beside them come hell or high water. Men tend to be competitive creatures in the Western world. I don't believe it's a core part of our nature, just an aspect of human potential that is encouraged if not figuratively beaten into us by our competition-based society. In any case, a lot of men sadly see other men as potential competitors and the sorriest of us can't seem to interact with another guy without thinking about who's coming up on top.

One result of this is that many men walk around wearing a façade of one sort or another, and when we get home, we want to be able to take that off and be ourselves. Prerequisite: a partner who will love and respect us when she sees us for who we truly are.

Fidelity. Simple word – big meaning. Most men want / demand fidelity in a partner. Perhaps due to the socio-biological need to ensure we are never cuckolded (i.e., unknowingly raising another male's offspring), most men value fidelity in their partners more than woman do.

With fidelity comes **unwavering commitment and faith**. Most men want a woman who commits to the integrity and growth of the relationship. It goes along with watching our backs when facing the raging horde, we want someone we can rely on and with whom we are moving in a desired direction through life. A core aspect of this that relates to masculine essence is the desire to have a woman who has faith in us, and who believes in our life mission. It goes along with the saying, "behind every great man there is an equally great woman who has faith in her partner."

Romance. Yes, I'm serious, but think *Bogey and Bacall,* or adventure movie romances. Sure, most of us do love getting flowers because of what they represent, and I suspect men are more prone to romantic folly than women. However, male romance is a little different from that of our feminine foils; flowers and verbal expressions of love and devotion are wonderful, but they may not have as much impact as actions, such as cooking a special meal, or a day of back country skiing. At their core, both are ways of expressing one's love and appreciation for the other, and a heartfelt commitment to engaging the life journey and dream together.

A self-sufficient, secure, and confident woman who has her own game to play. How else can a man know she is with him for who he is and not for his resources or some other less flattering motivation. The best partners are the same as the best companions in play and adventure – someone who can hold their own, carry their own gear, and can initiate the fun half the time. Having a tag-along in the game of life, love, and romance just doesn't cut it. It is also in the nature of such women to try to make men responsible for their happiness and there are few things more deadly to a relationship.

A woman who can ask for what she needs and wants.

Ever try to figure out how to please someone who won't talk? It's boring and onerous. Mind reading is for mentalists and other carnival acts; it has no place in the desired relationships of most men. Men want a partner who takes responsibility for her needs and desires and can communicate these with honesty, love, and respect; and, one who has no undue expectations that he is either going to meet her expectation or somehow fulfill her.

A woman who 'gets,' likes, and respects men. This is the hallmark of a Great Woman. Relationships can be a troubling maze when we first start the adventure of romance in adolescence, and for many it remains an "I don't get it yet but I'm working on it" process well into our twenties. I used to joke that men are not datable until their thirties but I came to realize that this is largely true of women as well – to make a long story short, few if any of us have negotiated the scene without at least a few scars – it's no wonder they call it the battle of the sexes.

Some of us tolerate the bumps and bruises of life better than others but there are many men and women who are battle-weary and gun-shy. A few opt out of the game altogether, but most suppress their fear and trudge on like dutiful soldiers of love. A few toughen up and become quite mercenary about the venture and some of them set out to get even. For them, it's a quest for what they can get from their partners, or a battle over who's on top.

Then there are the ones who stand out from the crowd. These are the men and women who have endured their fair share of hurt and disappointment in love but who harbour no grudges and do not allow their experiences to taint their views of the complementary gender. They are the courageous few that remain optimistic, give the best of themselves, and hope for the best in others. The feminine version – I call these the Great Women for they have an unshakable faith and liking for their male counterparts. Deep down, I believe most men want such a woman, though for many this desire lies unconscious.

A woman who knows how to treat a man – with loving dignity and respect. Ever hear a man say something like, "Oh, my wife won't let me do that," or a woman say something like, "Oh, he thinks he's golfing with his buddies this Sunday, but I'll set him straight when I get home"? Pitiful right? Sadly, this is the sort of dynamic to which far too many relationships fall prey.

I believe it starts out innocently enough in most cases; we all want to be cared for and most of us have memories of a loving, caring parent who'd comfort us when we were ill. This often plays out innocently in relationships by way of pet names, buying treats and toys (e.g., new iPod), emotional coddling when a partner is upset, but without a fundamental respect for the sovereignty and dignity of one's partner, it can degenerate quickly to parent-like control over the other.

It works both ways, of course, but from the male perspective, once a woman begins to treat him like a child or irresponsible adolescent, most men feel diminished and resentful. We want to be seen as a woman's hero and knight (in an evolved way at least), and when a partner matronizes us, we will long for and perhaps seek a female who sees us for the hero we are.

It doesn't work well for women either as they can end up feeling they have a child to care for rather than a mate. When I see this in married couples, it often turns out that the marriage is dead beyond resurrection.

The bottom line: most men want a woman to treat them like a prince or king, with dignity and respect, but also a woman who deserves and expects to be treated like a princess or queen.

No game play, manipulation, or drama. Most men really don't want mind games or drama in their lives. With the exception of psychopaths and players, we like to tell and hear it like it is, and begin to feel 'trapped' and resentful when partners try to draw us into their drama or use manipulation (e.g., the silent treatment, withholding sex). Drama may get the emotional juices flowing for a lot of women and some men, but for most of us it's an unwanted stress and a toxic bath for most relationships.

Great and Sexy Sex. There it is. Men may have a vestigial predisposition for a wandering eye, but as discussed above we are not prisoners of biology. Though most of us really want one special woman in our lives, we are still left with a deep desire to have sex, have it often, and to crave variety and an enthusiastic partner. Perhaps it is a way of satisfying the conditions that would exist were we out sowing wild oats: (frequent sex = many possible impregnations) + (variety = many partners) + (enthusiastic = new and/or ovulating partners) = Wow!

Quiet Bonding. Watch two women bonding and you'll likely hear a lot of talk, verbal sharing about a lot of everything and a lot of nothing. Watch two men bonding and you may see them playing a relatively silent game of pool together or fishing 50 feet apart on the same stream with nary a word between them. Sure, we verbally share as well, but we have a particular fondness of quiet or silent shared time and activity that a lot of women don't seem to get. Finding a woman who gets and practices this with us, along with a balance of verbal chatter, is an amazingly powerful feature in a union.

How Traditional Marriage Fails Men

There seems to be a consensus among researchers that men benefit physically and mentally from marriage.[24] Some would even suggest that men get a better deal than women from traditional marriage, but I believe the old model does fall short for men in important ways. I also believe the OYM will give them an even better deal and bring their beloved mates up to parity. What follows is a brief description of some of the ways I see contemporary marriage failing men.

Antiquated Bondage

The basis of traditional marriages dates back to the days when a man was supposed to take the responsibility for housing and feeding a woman from her father. In some cultures, the father was expected to pay the groom a form of compensation, called a dowry, for doing this. Back then, marriage wasn't just open-ended (permanent unless broken by divorce), it was "until death do you part." That wasn't a quaint vow of eternal love but a bond of responsibility, enforced by the powers of king and country.

At least in the Western world today, neither men nor women need be bound to each other by relatively permanent legal restraints as though their survival depended on it. That alone is good reason to question traditional marriage, but another is that the courts continue to be swayed by some of those old notions. Though they have come a long way in getting in step with social change, our legal systems are notoriously conservative and slow to modify and there are a lot of old folks who sit in the judge's seat who might tend to hold rather quaint and old-fashioned notions. The bottom line is that men still appear to be treated unfairly (unequally) by the court system in divorce decisions.

Economic Entrapment

Traditional marriage makes men more vulnerable to economic entrapment in a number of ways. The most

---

24. See - Lee A. Lillard and Constantijn W.A. Panis, "Marital Status and Mortality: The Role of Health," Demography, 33(3):313_327, 1996.

obvious being that it makes men targets for gold-, silver-, and bronze-diggers. Certainly successful women today are vulnerable to this as well, but it's still a largely female strategy for acquiring financial means. Even though men have an instinctive drive to provide and protect, it's one thing to do that for someone who loves you for who you are, and another for someone who wants you for what you have.

Sadly, you don't have to be wealthy to fall prey to this sort of parasitism these days. In a recent Ask Men issue it was pointed out that as the economy has slumped, these freeloaders have lowered their sights to the point where no one is immune.[25] Although one would hope you'd be able to spot one of these sweethearts before you reach the altar, men are sometimes notoriously bad at doing that and then a traditional marriage with all its legal implications becomes a financial trap.

Another path to economic entrapment lies in the decisions that couples tend to make when they are in a traditional marriage. When they assume permanence in the marriage and make major economic decisions as though being together was a foregone conclusion, they create financial vulnerabilities and dependencies that bind the couple together long after their love has died.

Overextended or excessively commingled finances, one partner forsaking a career (e.g., to focus on child-rearing), or simply becoming spoiled by the luxuries a dual income can sometimes afford; the end result is economic bondage. One of the most commonly cited reasons couples have expressed to me for staying in an unhappy union is that they cannot afford to live separately. Now how sad is that? Imagine having to give up a chance for love and happiness because you can't afford to be free of your current partner.

---

25. http://ca.askmen.com/dating/heidi_500/581_gold_digger_types.html

When a traditional marriage does end in divorce (over 50% do these days), if your partner has given up a career for the relationship with your blessings, guess what, there is still such a thing as spousal support, a.k.a. spousal maintenance, a.k.a. alimony. Although a dying phenomenon in this age of dual careers, it is still a factor to contend with if your partner quits a career or becomes underemployed as a result of the marriage. Since that is most frequently the female partner, men may still be saddled with spousal support upon divorce.

Probably the most contentious issue during divorces is who gets the kids. Sounds rather silly when written that way but it can become a vicious, bloody battle and unhappily, it's often the children who lose the most. In the confessional of psychotherapy, I've been privy to admissions of trying to sabotage a divorcing partner's reputation, career, and freedom through allegations of spousal abuse, child abuse or neglect, drug abuse and just about anything else that might sway a judge to deem the other party an unfit parent.

Although there are many reasons for such behaviour, none of which are excusable, I've come to the conclusion that in many cases it comes down to money. There is a saying I've heard bandied around by family law lawyers: "Where the children go, the money goes." Despite changes in the law in most jurisdictions that places men on an equal footing with women regarding child custody and access, the courts, for the same reasons mentioned earlier, still tend to favour women in this regard.

The bottom line: in a traditional marriage with children, should a man divorce his wife, he may face the substantial costs of supporting his children (and perhaps his former spouse) yet not get to enjoy fair access to them. If that isn't financial entrapment and emotional cruelty, what is?

Erosion of Sovereignty

A popular men's e-zine recently reported the results of a survey; responding readers identified the loss of identity as being the biggest downside of marriage. This is not an unfounded concern, for traditional marriage, with its assumptions of relative permanence and expectations that two become one, fosters just that. Men and women are both vulnerable to this but perhaps women more so. We don't get off any easier, however, as I'll explain below.

Traditional marriages encourage the partner dominated by feminine essence (usually the woman) to focus on the needs of the relationship, their partners, and eventually their children at the expense of themselves. The loss of self to the needs of others conflicts with a fundamental need to feel we have control over our own lives. Relinquishing sovereignty in this way gives rise to a need to regain some sense of control over life and that often leads to attempts to control the other partner.

The result can be a power struggle that can be so subtle it can go undetected for years. The worst outcome is that the other partner (usually the male) will surrender control and lose his own sovereignty to the collective. When that happens, it's game over I'm afraid – neither partner can be happy.

If you think this is an uncommon occurrence, think back to how many times you've heard men say such things as, "My wife would never let me," "I'll have to ask my wife," or "That's up to my wife?" Each is indicative, not of a respectful consideration of one's partner's wishes, but obedience to her authority.

How about the times you've heard a women say, "If my husband thinks X, Y, or Z, he has another thing coming," "He wanted to do it but I wouldn't let him," or my personal favourite (this was actually overheard in a Wal-Mart store) "He thinks that now, but after the wedding that's going to change." Wow! Holy relationship toxicity, Batman! Each of those is not a healthy self-assertion within joint decisions but a disrespectful if not contemptuous assertion of control.

Ironically, when it happens, men feel controlled and resentful and women lose their respect for and interest in their partners. It's lose-lose I'm afraid.

Dee's Advice: Don't lose yourself and give over your control; don't ever 'allow' your wife to 'let' you do things.

The One Year Marriage: A Man's New BFF?

The structure of the One Year Marriage is very consistent with the male perspective. Taking care of business first, setting the rules and boundaries that will ensure fairness and mutual benefit, is a propensity of the masculine. At the same time, doing so creates the space and support needed for the relationship to flourish and blossom – consistent with the feminine perspective.

One of the core benefits of a OYM is that it optimizes the probability that your union will bring you the sort of things you truly want from a relationship. Since you negotiate the conditions and expectations of the union with your beloved and get to renegotiate and renew it every year, if you're not getting what you deeply desire, then you're not doing it right. But let's examine how the OYM might address the areas where traditional marriage often fails men (and in most cases women equally).

Antiquated Bondage: Not applicable. As a freely negotiated, time-limited agreement that automatically dissolves on its anniversary according to an agreed-upon plan, the OYM is the antithesis of antiquated bondage. It honours both parties equally and provides the supportive structure that will help the relationship flourish, while maximizing individual rights and freedom.

Economic Entrapment: The OYM is an antidote to economic entrapment. Since both parties are compelled to mind their own financial interests and to make no decisions that assume the marriage will exist the same time next year, it's a strong remedy for the sort of decisions that bring about financial bondage. As for protection against diggers of gold, silver, and bronze, you may still fall prey to them during the dating phase of a relationship, but mention the OYM when things get serious and they'll quickly reveal themselves. They'll either refuse to even consider it or they'll disappear like a gambler's money.

Erosion of Sovereignty: The OYM is the best way I can imagine for two people to share themselves fully in a relationship while retaining their personal sovereignty. It honours the individuality of both partners and establishes conditions that help ensure that both retain it, and at the same time protects them from unnecessary, counter-productive vulnerabilities that could otherwise result in one or both partners withholding out of fear. The loss of personal identity is highly unlikely unless you really work at surrendering it.

Freedom. Can men have the freedom they crave and still be in a committed, loving relationship? Yes! The OYM promotes the freedom men instinctively desire, yet provides the structure that allows a full and rich love to flourish. In the worst-case scenario, if things go seriously south for either of you, there is a clean, respectful, win-win termination process. More important, by encouraging both parties to each retain their individuality and financial solvency, it diminishes or eliminates the conditions that generate controlling behaviours in marital unions. The result is that you will be freer to give fully of your self and enjoy doing just that as it will be a true gift of love, not an obligation.

What About Love? Love is at the top of the list for both men and women in what they want from their relationships. Love is both state and process and it happens or it doesn't for two people. The wise seeker of true love optimizes the chances for it to ignite, and sets the conditions for a great love to grow and endure.

As I stated earlier in the book, I believe the best means to finding a love that is deeply fulfilling is to evolve to sufficient completeness so that we lose the "need" for another. To yearn for a great love is wonderful and healthy, but to need someone to fill something we feel is lacking in our lives, is trouble in the waiting. When we approach a relationship this way, we cheat ourselves of the drive to develop those growing edges. At the same time, we place a terrible strain of unrealizable expectations on the bond with our partner, a strain that is likely to sabotage the very thing we desire most.

The desire to be able to stand alone is strong within the male psyche to begin with; strong to a fault at times, but it is only when we have that and the self-respect it engenders that we can enjoy a bond that is free and un-hindering. It is only then that we can relish in our partner's independence, rather than feeling threatened by it.

I also believe that men who evolve themselves to this point will also attract the highest quality partners, i.e., kindred spirits who have evolved and grown their independence. Become a prince and you will attract a princess. How does this relate to the OYM? For one, less evolved women may not buy into the concept – they may be too aligned with societal norms and expectations. By embracing the OYM concept, you'll likely weed them out.

Finally, embracing the OYM concept will support you in

your continued growth and development as a person and as a man. The OYM requires a mature and independent personality, and demands that we maintain that and not regress into a lower state. If a man and woman evolve themselves into a king and a queen, each independent with his and her own realm to rule, they will attract each other. Coming together in a OYM will help prevent the king from becoming a jester, and the queen a scullery maid.

Chapter 5

And Then There Were Three...Four...

"All of us have moments in our lives that test our courage. Taking children into a house with a white carpet is one of them." ~ *Erma Bombeck*

When Children Arrive... Is a OYM Still Viable?

Most couples find that when children come along, it turns their world upside down. A new father once told me that he had been warned repeatedly that children would demand more of him and his wife than they could possibly imagine, and they would have to change their lives more than they could anticipate. He went on to say that despite his vivid imagination and a healthy dose of negative expectations, their first child demanded more of him and his wife and changed their lives more than either had expected. Then he added that it was a wonderful experience, one he wouldn't trade for anything.

The Hierarchy of Care

There is no denying it, when a couple has a child, as much as it might be an act of love and something to enrich their lives, it creates high demands on time and energy, and the needs of children, unlike our own, can't be put off for very long. I believe this is the primary reason why many couples make one of the most common and serious mistakes in their relationships: they place the needs of their children ahead of their own.

I realize that statement might rankle a few readers but stick with me on this for a moment. What is it they tell you to do during the pre-flight briefing on planes in the event that the cabin loses pressure? *Put your own mask on first before trying to assist a child or another adult near you.* There is good reason for this – if you try to help someone else first, especially a child who might not be able to help you in return, you risk passing out before you can get back to yourself, in which case both of you could perish. The simple fact of life is that...

> *...as an adult, no one but you can know what you need to do to stay healthy and happy, and no one but you can take responsibility for ensuring that.*

In a relationship without children, you owe it to yourself and to your partner to make your needs your highest priority. I don't mean that in a selfish "me only" way, but in a gentle, giving way of remaining aware of what your needs are and taking the responsibility to ensure they are met. No one can do that for you and if you fail in that one vital responsibility, you and your partner will suffer the consequences. When both partners take responsibility for first ensuring their own health and happiness, they will be more available, physically and emotionally, for each other and the needs of the relationship.

When children come along, greater stress for both of you is inevitable and it becomes all the more important that taking care of one's self remains the highest priority of both. The children's needs come next, right? No, not yet. Your partner and the relationship should remain the next highest priority. When couples make the health and happiness of their relationship their next highest priority, they are more likely to end up a healthy, happy couple, and have the physical and emotional well-being to be fully available to their children. What better gift is there to give children than two happy healthy parents in a loving relationship? In fact, I'd like to suggest that if children are brought up in that sort of environment, most everything else falls into place naturally.

Many parents today lavish their children with more material comforts than children could have dreamed of just a few generations ago. Countless toys, media players, gaming systems, computers, and even cell phones are common in the arsenal of many of today's children. On top of that, there are designer or otherwise fashionable clothes for kids to stay on top of. Then there is a legion of lessons of one sort or another that many parents rush their kids to.

I'm not alone in suspecting that all this material attention is having a negative impact on our children; intuitively, we can see it on a daily basis. To name a few: concentration and attention problems; low frustration tolerance; reduced capacity to delay gratification; low appreciation for the value of things; and entitlement issues. We want the best for our children, to make certain they are happy and grow into healthy, happy adults, but I can guarantee you that all the material junk in the world isn't going to do that, nor are the skating, piano, or dance lessons. If not, what is?

An associate of mine once took a trip to Africa with her church and made an interesting discovery while they toured villages each day. What she saw were women who invariably greeted the busload of visitors with wide happy smiles and invited them into their huts. She saw village men and women working together harmoniously, singing as they went about their chores and all the while laughing children ran and played in every direction. In one village, the only toy the children had was a partially deflated soccer ball that they joyfully shared. She had never witnessed such an intact sense of community or seen such happy children.

To her surprise, the reactions of her fellow tourists were very different; they would often shed tears and lament how terrible the children had it – mud floors, straw beds, and no toys. Most did not seem to notice how happy the children were or how harmonious their world was. Blindness comes in many forms.

What that shared tale reaffirmed for me was that you can literally raise happy and healthy children in a grass hut with mud floors, a straw bed, and no toys, as long as their sense of being loved by and securely connected to their caregivers is strong. So how can we give that to our children? Give them two healthy, happy parents in a loving relationship. Start with yourself; ensure you are happy and healthy – this is your number one priority. Next, assist your partner in his or her own health and happiness and ensure your relationship remains vibrant and loving. Finally, give your children the most precious thing you have to offer – your love and your time.

When we do otherwise, when we sacrifice our own needs for that of our children, when our attention is diverted from our partners, we erode the very core of what children need most. I've heard countless tales of how a relationship began to deteriorate when children became part of the household. It's easy to see how that happens: like other demands on the 'busyness' side of the relationship coin, not attending to the needs of children often has immediate consequences. Also, our instinctive inclination to nurture the young and needy is near irresistible. Given the countless possible demands a child or two can place on parents, it's easy to see how we can give too much for too long.

The alternative is not denying children what they truly need, it's a matter of remaining clear about just what 'need' means and remaining aware of the health and happiness of self and partnership. Certainly children will take an amazing amount of time and energy from you both, but if you're not committed to preserving the core of the family unit as your highest priority, they can easily take more time and energy than you have to give and that is a lose-lose-lose situation.

Still unclear? Let me stick some arbitrary numbers to it. If it takes a minimum of, say, 10 quality hours a week to maintain yourself and another 10 hours of quality time with your mate to maintain your relationship, then you can put in the roughly 37 hours a week it takes to attend to the needs of a child. On top of a 40- to 50-hour work and commute week, that seems like a lot but remember, you have about 112 hours per week in which to do all of this.

The point here is this: you can put a load of time into caring for a young child without compromising your self or your relationship, as long as you never allow those demands to cut into the 20 hours or so of self and relationship time. As a couple, you must remain the centre of the family, like two suns forming a double star system, and the children must be accepted and loved as your satellites.

Is a OYM Compatible with Children?

Many people I've spoken to object to the idea of a OYM because they see it as precluding having children. Alternately, some people hold onto the view that once a couple does have children they are obligated to remain together for the sake of the children. A November 18, 2010 *Time*/Pew poll found that 59% of respondents described having children as an important reason for getting married in the first place. So does having children affect the viability of doing a OYM? The short answer is, not at all.

Concerning the first objection mentioned above, it is entirely possible to do a marriage by one-year contracts and have children. Remember, the contract is renewable – a OYM is not a commitment to separate in one year; it is a commitment to examine the relationship, decide what is working and not working, and then 'renegotiate' and commit for another year. Only when a win-win agreement cannot be forged in time does the marriage automatically dissolve. As I've argued throughout this book, this process is more likely to result in a happier and more satisfied couple and hence a more secure union.

For couples that believe that a marriage must stay intact once children become part of the picture, there are a couple of things to consider. One is the growing body of evidence that refutes the notion that divorce is necessarily harmful to children, which I'll discuss in more detail shortly. The other is that allowing the marital union to dissolve, even if you decide the contract is not working for you, is only an option. You always have the right to decide to stay together 'for the sake of the children,' though I would argue that you would not be doing them much of a favour by that.

Children and Divorce

One of the issues that come up in my discussions about the OYM is the impact that the dissolution of a OYM might have on children. Two commonly expressed concerns are: 1. A OYM is more likely to be short-term than a traditional marriage; and 2. Children will be negatively impacted more by the resulting family instability.

Regarding longevity, that's an issue that cannot yet be addressed; the OYM is a new concept and so there is no data to analyze. My belief is, however, that the OYM approach would result in longer, happier unions than the traditional approach, but at a minimum will last at least as long. That's not a hard benchmark to beat – divorce is the end point in roughly 50% of traditional marriages anyway, and having children appears to only moderately reduce the divorce rate.[26] Even then, it's only when the children are of preschool age that divorce rates are affected; the presence of school-age

---

26. E.g., Aandrew Cherlin, "The effect of children on marital dissolution," Demography ©, Vol. 14, #3, 1977-AUG, Pages 265 to 272.

children appears to have no effect.

Side-stepping here a moment, there are some disturbing statistics regarding children, divorce, and parent loss. The ill effects of a child not having contact with his or her father after divorce are quite serious,[27] and it has been estimated that 77% of non-custodial fathers were unable to visit with their children as ordered by the courts because of interference by the custodial parent, which is apparently three times the rate of non-compliance with court-ordered child support.[28]

This is just the tip of the iceberg, but what the stats in the above two paragraphs convey to me is that: a) people with children in traditional marriages divorce as much as those with no children; and b) over half of traditional marital dissolutions are done so poorly that they result in parental loss. So by my reading of this, traditional marriage does not appear to provide children with much security at all. In any case, as mentioned above, should a OYM dissolve, you will always have the option of remaining together 'for the sake of the children,' the folly of which I'll discuss below.

The Impact of Divorce

So what is the intrinsic impact of divorce on children? A lot of research into this has been done over the years and a number of reviews of the research have concluded that divorce does have a negative impact on children. Unfortunately, by my reading of the literature, the results of the vast majority of studies are 'correlational,' which means you cannot claim that parental divorce causes whatever differences are found in children from divorced versus intact families.

---

27. See - http://www.photius.com/feminocracy/facts_on_fatherless_kids.html
28. J.A. Vanini & E. Nichols. "Visitational Interference - A National Study" (Originally published Sept. 1992)

More importantly, the studies are badly 'confounded,' meaning there are too many factors (e.g., amount and nature of parental conflict, ease of divorce, quality of co-parenting relationship, etc.) that are not teased out, meaning that the results are unable to suggest why children may be affected the way they appear to be.

In my professional opinion, the most serious flaw in these studies is they fail to compare the psychosocial well-being of children of divorced parents with the only meaningful comparison group – children of intact families whose parents are unhappy enough to divorce, but who stay together 'for the sake of the children' or other reasons. A few studies have found, however, that children of divorced parents who do not conflict, do better than children of married parents who do conflict. Again, these are only correlational studies but they do suggest that divorce may be a better option for children in some cases.

A review of the literature is not my intent here, but I do want to dispel the popular notion that divorce is necessarily harmful to children. To begin with, even if the results of review studies that do suggest a harmful effect were reliable, the effects are actually rather small; most children from divorced families do quite well.

A growing number of studies have teased out some of the factors that appear to mitigate poor adjustment that some children do exhibit following divorce.[29] [30] These include:

- Parental Conflict: As you might expect, children who have been exposed to high level of parental conflict have more problems than children whose parents do not conflict, whether the parents are divorced or remain

29. E.g., Amato, P. R. (1993). Children's adjustment to divorce: Theories, hypotheses, and empirical support. Journal of Marriage and the Family, 55, 23-38.
30. Kelly, J. B., & Emery, R. E. (2003). Children's adjustment following divorce: Risk and resiliency perspectives. Family Relations, 52, 352-362.

together.

- Parental Adjustment and Well-Being: Children whose parents are emotionally healthy and well adjust to divorce do better than children whose parents are not.

- Parental Loss: Children who lose contact with a parent enough to compromise that relationship after divorce fair less well than those who are able to maintain a good relationship with both parents.

- Distressing Change: The greater the amount of distressing change following divorce, the greater the likelihood of a poor adjustment in children. This includes such things as being forced to change friends, schools, habits, etc.

There is much more information on the Net on this issue and there are some excellent discussion pages to be found for those so interested. I invite you to explore the scientific basis for all this by doing a little research on your own, but be forewarned, it is in the nature of scientific research to see the results of studies that appear to contradict each other. It has much to do with the questions researchers ask in the first place and how they go about trying to find the answers, but I think it is fair to say that there is a truth in most valid studies – it's just a matter of figuring out what the results actually mean.

My summary of it all is this: under the best of circumstances, divorce can be stressful on children, but with parental diligence, it can be minimized, and long-term ill effects can be avoided. What they can do to help their children successfully negotiate a divorce include:

- Don't conflict openly;

- Continue to demonstrate respect for each other;

- Talk to the children about the severance, address their

fears and questions, and reassure them they will always have both parents;

- Share custody and access as equally as feasible;

- Commit to a win-win separation and divorce, and a respectful if not loving co-parenting alliance;

- Never say anything bad about the other parent as this is tantamount to emotional abuse of the child;

- Keep yourself healthy and happy, regardless of the circumstance.

If you know people who have gone through a divorce, you may already realize that those steps are often not followed before, during, and after the severance of a marriage. From my vantage point as a psychologist, I've been privy to the living hell parents often feel compelled to put their children through when they are in the midst of a divorce. Driven by anger and fear, parents who love their children often do poorly by them when caught up in the trauma of divorce.

That is not to say that people don't divorce from traditional marriages in healthy, loving ways, but that seems to be the exception, not the rule. Why? Is it a matter of parents not loving their children enough? I don't think so.

The sad truth is that divorce can bring the absolute worst out in people. Mature, reasonable adults can find themselves regressing into angry, vindictive, 'children' who are out to get all the toys and make their partners pay. Separation can trigger deeply buried feelings of abandonment that have the ability to overwhelm an adult's better sensibilities. This is too easily encouraged by well-meaning friends and family who often feel they need to take sides. More destructive is the effect the legal system has on divorcing couples.

The legal system in North America is an adversarial one.

It is based on criminal justice where one side argues the guilt of a defendant and the other side argues the innocence. Out of the ensuing battle comes a decision: guilty or not guilty. It is simply not well equipped by process or tradition to peacefully resolve disputes and generate win-win outcomes. The result – divorce can easily degenerate into a blood sport.

I have a friend who is a multi-business owner and venture capitalist. He once advised me never to get lawyers involved in a business deal until the papers are ready to be drawn up. In his considerable experience, *lawyers are deal-breakers, not deal-makers*. However, lawyers are often the first people couples turn to when seeking divorce. Big mistake.

When a couple goes to court, even if they have good intentions in the first place, it's as though they are accompanied by a hired gunslinger (the lawyer), armed with a multitude of financial assaults sanctioned by the legal system. It only takes one false move on the part of either party and a gun battle rages. Unfortunately the only parties ever injured are the soon-to-be ex-partners and their children. Add to that the fact that the poorer the job a lawyer does (if a quick and peaceful settlement is your goal), the more he or she gets paid, and you have a system set up for painful, adversarial ordeals.

That is not to say that all lawyers are only interested in their billable hours. I've had the pleasure of knowing some great ones both as friends and colleagues (and more recently, a niece), and I know that many are as weary of the insanity of traditional divorce as their clients.

The other reality of traditional divorce, because it is based on a win-lose philosophy, is that there can be real financial winners and losers. I know people who have become near destitute following divorce. Most people know this or are soon advised of such by friends or lawyers.

Put it all together and it looks like this: two people, who we can assume are not on the best of terms to begin with, enter into a legal severance negotiation (divorce). The emotional and financial stakes are big and both parties have likely been advised and encouraged by friends, family, and lawyers, to make certain they get what is coming and don't get taken. Emotions are running high and may include both fear and anger, and one or more of the parties may have psychologically regressed into a more childlike state of mind. What do you get? You get the blood sport of modern divorce, of course. Is it any wonder children are sometimes caught in the crossfire?

I've known a lot of people who, being hurt, angry, and scared in the midst of divorce, act in ways in which they would never have believed themselves capable. When this happens, both adults pay for it emotionally and financially, and the children frequently get caught in the gears, and perhaps suffer the most. Justice Harvey Brownstone, a family court judge, wrote an amazing book on the matter that I highly recommend.[31]

Children, Divorce, and the OYM

How can we prevent this? Well, what if a couple had the wisdom to decide ahead of time, while they were in love and wanted the best for each other, what the healthiest and most fair way to dissolve their union would be? What if they then created an inviolable contract that would have little success of being challenged in court, that assured each that their agreed-upon plan would be honoured in the event of the unthinkable? Can you think of a greater gift of compassion and love to your partner and future children? That is an integral part of a OYM.

---

31. Harvey Brownstone (2009). Tug of War: A Judge's Verdict on Separation, Custody Battles, and the Bitter Realities of Family Court. ECW Press, Toronto.

So then how would the severance of a OYM compare in its impact on children?

- There would likely be minimal conflict since the union will have undergone yearly reviews and renegotiations, thereby eliminating hot spots that often boil for years;

- There would be nothing to conflict over regarding the terms of the severance since that would have all been decided and contracted while the couple was still in love and wanting the best for each other;

- Fundamental respect between parents will likely remain intact because each has continued to honour the other and nurture the relationship;

- The economic well-being of both parents will be optimized (if they have minded their own business) thereby reducing fears about the future;

- Each parent will have an intact sense of independence and sovereignty, thereby minimizing fear and anger, and optimizing happiness;

- The parents will better be able to come together in support of their children during the severance and will be primed to forge a win-win, healthy co-parenting agreement.

I believe that if a couple opts for a OYM, follows the spirit of it throughout their relationship, and later decides not to renew it, they are in the best possible position to do justice by themselves and their shared children, resulting in minimal risk of long-term ill effects all around.

Let me repeat something once again. Parents and prospective parents who are considering following a OYM model should keep this in mind: separating, even if you decide the contract is not working for you, is only an option. You always have the right to decide to stay together either in a default common-law marriage or you can even opt for a traditional marriage.

Special Considerations

Children will complicate your life and it is no surprise that it will complicate your OYM agreement. The following are a few considerations that may impact the OYM.

Parenting Issues

There are a lot of issues that parents are wise to discuss before pregnancy that relate to parenting styles and philosophies, and your hopes for your children. For example, will you provide a permissive atmosphere or one with boundaries? What sorts of behavioural consequences are deemed appropriate for bad behaviour? How much TV and video gaming will the children be allowed to access? Will the children be schooled at home, in the public system, or privately? Will they have chores and at what age?

Parenting differences are one of the most common stressors cited by partners experiencing marital distress, right behind difficulties with finances and intimacy. There are dozens of such issues that can seriously impact your relationship if you find yourselves at odds over them. Further, your children will not only know it, they'll take full advantage of it to drive a wedge into parental authority in order to create more freedom in the resulting void.

It's not my purpose here to discuss any of these in detail, but being aware that differences between marital partners on parenting issues can be a serious problem and they'd best be discussed and resolved prior to having a child.

Business Issues

Some of the 'business' issues you and your partner might want to discuss ahead of time include:

- Will one or both of you take time away from your careers to care for the child after he or she is born? If so, who will do so and for how long? How might that impact your careers and how will the impact be rebalanced?

- If there is an anticipated shift in incomes, because of the above, what changes will be needed in the way you share financial responsibilities?

- Exactly how will you share the countless parenting duties to ensure the two of you shoulder equal loads in doing life together?

- Should one or both of you decide not to renew your agreement and vows at some point, how will you honour each other and your children during and after the severance? What is in your and your children's best interests and how will that be written into your next agreement?

Each of these issues should be discussed and decided upon while keeping in mind that the relationship may no longer be in place at the same time next year. As unlikely as that may seem at the time, it is vital that the possibility of marital dissolution be acknowledged and taken into consideration in all of your choices.

Does that sound pessimistic? Does it seem as though it would take the joy out of planning a child? Well, it shouldn't, any more than creating a fire plan would compromise your enjoyment of your home, having a career backup plan would spoil the joys of your career, or writing a Last Will and Testament would reduce your enjoyment of life. The planning for dissolution that is the hallmark of the OYM reminds me of the principles of good seamanship and military planning: commit to the best desired outcome, but always be prepared for the worst. That approach to marriage could result in a greater sense of solidarity that the two of you could take on such a difficult task successfully, and in a greater sense of security, knowing that in the worst-case scenario, all will be well for both of you.

A Final Note

You might ask yourself what you'll be modeling for your children should you decide to raise them within a OYM. I certainly have. Would you be teaching them that nothing lasts in life so don't ever count on anything, or to accept impermanence? Would you be teaching them that relationships only come down to a legal contract, or that mutually agreed-upon boundaries are important in them? Would they learn that relationships are not secure, or that true security comes from within? The answer depends on your current perspective, on your beliefs, and attitudes. The vessel of the OYM can either be half empty or half full.

Chapter 6

Resistance, Toxic Waste, & Other Great Opportunities

"Every therapeutic cure, and still more, any awkward attempt to show the patient the truth, tears him from the cradle of his freedom from responsibility and must therefore reckon with the most vehement resistance." ~ *Alfred Adler*

Resistance: An Opportunity in Disguise

Resistance to change is natural. Changes in our world compel us to adjust to them or adjust against them and research shows that such change, whether desirable or undesirable, is stressful to some degree. That's not a bad thing when you consider that all growth – physical, mental, emotional, or spiritual – is a form of adaptation to some internal or external challenge. How we respond to challenges can determine whether we grow or simply maintain the status quo.

Rational and emotional resistance to the OYM concept is expected for most readers because it contradicts our cultural beliefs about what marriage and commitment are supposed to look like. I believe any time we hear something that contradicts our beliefs, we ought to question it; beliefs are an important part of the lens we place on our experience, the lens that determines our interpretation of reality. If there is too much flexibility in our beliefs, if they are too easily displaced, our sense of reality and hence our psychological stability may be compromised. On the other hand, if our beliefs are not open to examination and revision, then our sense of reality can become antiquated and unable to serve us well. Simply dismissing different or troubling ideas robs us of an opportunity to grow through altering or reaffirming our beliefs.

Resistance to the idea of entering an unfettered marriage bond may also be due to factors that warrant challenge – insecurities, mistrust of others, hoping to find someone to complete us, or hoping to find financial security through a mate. By exploring any resistance you might experience, you can uncover growing edges that are vital to your personal development and to finding a deep and abiding love.

Common Objections

I've listed a handful of common objections to the OYM that I've fielded in my discussions with colleagues, clients, friends, and strangers on planes. I've included them to provide examples of how the reality of a OYM, once the fog of misunderstanding and fear is lifted, can often address our fears and concerns. Although I could write pages about each objection, I've kept my responses short and simple. If you have objections that you want to express, feel free to direct them to 'oneyearmarriage@gmail.com', and I will address them through the OYM blog on my website, 'gsrenfrey.com'.

I would not feel secure in a marriage if it were easy and pain-free for my partner to leave me. This is a common concern, more often expressed by women, sometimes in the form of "I could never fully give of myself if I thought my partner might walk away in a year." It speaks to one of the more damaging consequences of traditional marriage – many rely on the legal and emotional difficulty involved in leaving a marriage to provide them with some assurance that their partner will stick around. The questions I usually pose to this are: "Is that what you really want – to be with someone against his or her will or preference?" "What are you basing or hoping to base your sense of security on?"

The OYM is founded on two interdependent lovers who support each other in their individual and collective paths in life. Never surrendering sovereignty or the capacity to go it alone, it promotes true, internally-referenced security, the only form that is real and reliable. Internally referenced security – that deeply held conviction that regardless of what life might bring, you will weather it well and emerge just fine—is the only form of security any of us can truly rely on. By looking to someone else, or to an institution like marriage to provide security, you're building a house of cards.

We're already too much of a disposable society – once we lose interest in something, we toss it away and replace it with something newer and shinier. Isn't the OYM just another step in that direction? No it is not. There is a difference between creating material objects with built-in obsolescence, and forging a relational agreement with a sunset clause. One represents a wasteful, environmentally harmful practice for economic gain; the other compels parties to uphold a win-win, mutually desired agreement.

Further, I do not believe it is closely related to our modern tendency to crave novelty. Yes, many people do buy new cars because they're tired of the old ones; many buy new clothes every season to remain "in fashion;" and many people spend a lot of money to have the latest techno-gadgets or other diversions. Tossing away things that are perfectly good is a sign of our addictive times, but the OYM is entirely unrelated to that.

Put simply, the OYM is a means to help ensure that the only thing that binds two people together is the love they share and their desire to continue to accompany each other on life's journey. If someone has difficulty maintaining his or her love for another and wants to replace that person once the infatuation phase has passed, then they need much more than this book. Riddle me this: if you ever found yourself saddled with such a partner, would you not rather discover that after one or two one-year agreements and be able to end things without complications, or learn of it after years of traditional marriage, perhaps by way of an affair, and face the pain and complication of a traditional divorce?

The OYM is also a recognition that people sometimes do change or otherwise grow apart despite their best efforts and should it ever become necessary to part ways, it helps to ensure it is done by way of a win-win formula that both parties have created in the spirit of love and respect. None of that to me sounds like something that promotes marital disposability.

Viewing marriage as a business agreement seems terribly unromantic. The world is already too businesslike; I don't want my most intimate personal relationship to be just another contract. Make no mistake, like it or not, traditional marriage is already a legal contract and business arrangement. If you doubt that, ask anyone who is in the midst of a divorce. Rather than ignore reality, a bad life strategy in general, the OYM compels us to recognize and deal with it. In that, it empowers us to choose to do the business side of things consciously, the way we desire, rather than the way social mores or the courts dictate, or worse yet, to do it unconsciously slipshod manner.

As for romance, I find the OYM to be deeply romantic. It is placing your heart and soul on the line when nothing but your mutual desire to be with each other binds the two of you together. It takes courage of heart and a high degree of faith to put it all on the line like that without the semi-permanent and legally binding contract of traditional marriage. I find the OYM to be romantic in the tradition of the great romances of fact and fiction.

How can one live in a committed relationship with the realization that the union may well dissolve in a matter of months? The answer is deceptively complex in its simplicity: a moment at a time. In so many ways, the OYM is consistent with Zen living, a core principle of which is to live without undue expectations. In Zen relationships, the key is to live without presumed or unilateral expectations of one's partner. As discussed in chapter one, these are the expectations that form from our wants without our partners ever agreeing to them. There is a deeper meaning to this, however.

In his best-selling book, *Tuesdays with Morrie*,[32] Mitch Albom beautifully conveys the wisdom of his dying teacher's last lessons. Among them is the suggestion to make death and the impermanence of things allies to help you get the most from life. None of us know whether we will be alive next year, next month, or even tomorrow. Accepting that and remaining conscious of it can be our greatest resource to making certain we do what we need to do in this life, today, to live completely. In the same manner, not 'expecting' or 'relying' on one's marriage to be there this time next year can help us truly appreciate what we have with our partner and keep it high on our priorities list.

If an important part of the OYM is not being entirely certain we will still be together after the anniversary, how can we plan anything for our future? How can we even plan a long-range vacation together? Is planning a bad thing? Planning for the future can be a joyous and important part of any relationship. If planning is short term, as in planning a special evening or weekend with your mate, it can create healthy positive intentions and expectations that can help ensure the relationship remains fresh and growing. You can also plan for the longer term, say a special vacation next year that happens to take place after the anniversary. Even longer

---

32. Mitch Albom (1997). Tuesdays with Morrie. Random House, New York.

term planning, such as buying a house together, can be done, as long as you make all such choices consciously and with needed safeguards.

The upshot is this – you can recognize the reality of impermanence, and still plan ahead as long as it is done with a degree of awareness that life has a way of altering the best laid out plans.

A OYM may work for childless couples, but would be unworkable and irresponsible once children become part of the picture; children need the security of a traditional marriage. I agree that children do best in a stable, happy home, but I don't believe traditional marriages are in any way better at providing that. To begin with, the Western tradition of the nuclear family is not the only viable way to raise healthy, happy children who grow up to be fulfilled adults and good human beings.

I've addressed a lot of this in the last chapter but I will quickly repeat a few important points here. By my readings, most of the research into the effects of divorce on children is badly confounded (i.e., essentially invalid). What they don't take into consideration are such factors as the degree of conflict between separating parents and the healthiness of the ensuing co-parenting relationship. In addition, I've not heard of a study that has used the only valid comparison group – children whose parents are unhappy enough to divorce but who stay together for one reason or another.

I would like to see the results of a study comparing the psychosocial welfare of children from unhappy marriages with those whose parents divorced without conflict, and support each other in their co-parenting responsibilities. My money is on the kids in the latter situation, and I believe a OYM is far more likely to give rise to healthy and loving co-parenting than traditional marriage and divorce.

The bottom line is this: children do best in a happy stable environment. The question remains, which is happier and more stable – a home with two unhappy parents who remain together out of obligation, or two homes with a happy parent in each who have a healthy, effective co-parenting relationship?

Again, my money is on the latter and this is why. The greatest gift parents can give their children is two happy parents in a loving relationship. Give them that and almost everything else falls together naturally. The problem with remaining together when unhappy is that children always know the truth; they sense it in their bones and feel it in their hearts. Children are very perceptive and if parents think they are able to hide their unhappiness from them, they're fooling only themselves.

What you give your children by remaining in an unhappy marriage are two unhappy parents in a non-loving relationship. Contrast that with children having two happy, independent parents who share a respectful co-parenting relationship and who have two loving homes to enjoy. The comparison doesn't even take into consideration the higher likelihood of children being exposed to parental conflict in the former.

Understanding Your Resistance to the OYM

If you have strong negative reactions to the one-year-marriage, you may learn a lot about yourself and your relationship preferences if you explore and articulate the reasons why. One key to doing this is to remain in more of a cognitive, intellectual frame. It's not that your emotional reactions are not important, for they are; it's just that emotions are notoriously capricious and difficult to understand. It's also hard to learn from them unless you can dig beneath the surface to discover their genesis.

Strong negative emotions are most often based on fear or pain. A reaction to something not immediately threatening, such as reading about the OYM, usually indicates that some value or principle you hold dear is being threatened or violated.

To understand negative reactions to the OYM, it is best to accept your emotions for what they are and then investigate them rationally. Asking yourself questions such as, "Does this violate or threaten something I hold dear?" is a good start. When you identify one or more such things, then you can go deeper by asking yourself what is important about them.

For example: let's say the whole idea of a OYM makes you angry. You explore those feelings and identify, "it violates the sanctity of marriage," and "it lacks true commitment," as two objections beneath your ire. Now you can examine what is important about a religiously sanctioned marriage and what true commitment means to you. Why do this? Well, as Socrates said…

"An unexamined life is not worth living"

Knowing why you think and feel the way you do is the essence of self-awareness, which is in turn, the cornerstone of an effective and meaningful life.

Another reason for exploring your deeper values and desires is that it can result in expanding your life and the options before you. Most of our desires stem from a handful of basic human needs, such as a need to be warm (having one's physical needs met), safe (being safe from eminent harm), and happy (experiencing joy, belonging, and love, etc.). Whether you want to conquer the world or just your golf swing, dig beneath that yearning and you'll discover a more fundamental desire or basic human need. Imagine how much better human history would have been if mass murderers such as Julius Caesar, Genghis Khan, and Adolph Hitler had realized that they only really wanted a sense of acceptance and belonging. Imagine the wondrous transformation the world would undergo if enough people came to that realization today.

Recognizing your core desires can help you put things in proper perspective; if your golf swing never quite gets there, you're less likely to bend your club or yourself out of shape if you realize that perfecting it was only a means to feeling happy. It can also provide you with other options; in case the 'conquer the world' thing doesn't quite work out, you can always work on your golf swing.

A good example of the examination process is provided in exploration two of the appendix. By exploring your resistance to the OYM this way, you can learn more about your deeper desires and you may even discover that the OYM might not only provide you with what you want from a partnership, but do so better than its traditional counterpart. In any case, it could generate some fairly interesting discussions between you and a prospective partner.

Toxic Waste – Of a Personal Nature

In the sections that follow, I address a number of attitudes, behaviours, and conditions that have a toxic effect on our emotional well-being and relationships. I've included this because some of the issues may impact your openness to a OYM and all of them will affect your or your partner's capacity to create and maintain a healthy, happy relationship. I do believe a OYM would help people eliminate these toxins from their lives as it would quickly bring them into focus and ensures they remain on the front burner. If you're committed to a traditional marriage, however, you are particularly advised to watch for these in yourself or your partner and take care of them prior to tying the knot – it will be much harder taking care of them afterwards.

Toxic waste; we hear about it every day – the nuclear and chemical by-products of our industrial lifestyle that threaten the very ecosystem that sustains us. If you want an idea of your own contribution to it, try this: for one month, do not flush your toilets, drain your sinks or shower, or dispose of any trash. Unless you're living an unusually sustainable lifestyle, I can guarantee you your home will become near unliveable in that time. We've become unaware of our impact on the environment (our biological home) because we've adopted 'sanitizing' practices that afford us the illusion that once waste is flushed, drained, or taken away, it is no longer a problem – out of sight, out of mind.

What many of us don't realize is that we can also generate vast amounts of relationship toxins without being aware of it. Just like physical waste, it can accumulate until our shared life-space (relationship) becomes unliveable.

Relationship toxins come in many forms but I've clustered them below in several broad categories. The essential characteristic of them is that each is something we think or do that erodes the quality of the shared life-space with our partners, either for ourselves, our partners, or both. Each is also completely controllable; therefore, preventable and correctable.

My reasons for including this discussion here are twofold: 1. These toxins can prevent couples from having a healthy relationship, and 2. Individuals who exhibit any of these tendencies have a greater likelihood of objecting to the concept of the OYM because of them.

It's not my intent here to give a complete list of relationship toxins and then provide biblio-therapy for them. Rather, I've identified some of the more common and destructive forms I've seen in distressed couples, and in individuals with serious relationship issues. The point of doing so is this: whether or not you are considering a OYM, if you or your prospective partner exhibit any of these it should be a yellow flag – you and / or your partner may not be ready for a healthy relationship. If you or your partner exhibit two of more of these, then I strongly advise you not to consider any sort of marriage until you correct the problems.

Toxic Beliefs and Attitudes

For our purposes, toxic beliefs and attitudes are enduring thought patterns and predispositions that compromise the cooperative spirit and emotional bond between two people. Their number is legion but their essential nature and impact are the same – they promote win-lose solutions to life's inevitable challenges, and generate negative feelings.

You don't have to use much imagination to see how these toxins work to produce discord and negativity. Here are a few of my favourites.

1. *Any un-negotiated, non-agreed on expectation of your partner:* These are the expectations of your partner that you create without his or her clear awareness and expressed agreement. On the giving end, this is making a demand on your partner that, if unheeded, will likely result in anger and blame. On the receiving end, it is having an obligation forced on you with the same emotional consequences. It's a lose-lose.

2. *Believing that you have the right to allow or disallow your partner to do things:* This is one of the most damaging beliefs possible. It is based on fundamental disrespect for your partner as an adult and a presumption of authority you simply do not or should not have. Men and women displaying this are controlling and tend to

lose interest in their partners if successful at it. Those who give in to this are diminished and end up resentful of their partners. It's a lose-lose.

3. *Believing that you need your partner's permission to do something you want to do:* This is the natural corollary of #2. There is everything right about checking in with your partner to see if what you want to do conflicts with made plans – that's being a courteous partner. Neither you nor your partner need each other's permission to follow your dreams or desires, so long as doing so does not compromise something consciously agreed-upon.

4. *Believing your partner has no right to privacy in thought or conversation:* This one includes email. Believing that your partner does not have the right to privacy or to speak to whomever she or he wants is terribly controlling and insecure. In this age of easy communication, it has given rise to such offensive behaviours as reading partner's emails and checking their cell phones to find out who they've been in touch with. It happens often and is always damaging. If this is one of your tendencies, then get a grip and stop it.

5. *Believing your partner has no right to personal time, or activities and friends outside of the relationship:* Another form of insecurity-based disrespect, this has the effect of shrinking your partner's world and the end product is always negative. Stop this insanity before it's too late.

6. *Wanting your partner to change:* This refers to wanting your partner to alter who he or she is, or to change something that is important to him or her. It is normal to run into friction points in any relationship and wanting and negotiating behavioural change is critical to resolving those, but outside of small behavioural tweaks, if you can't accept your partner just as he or she is, you have no business being in a relationship with each other.

7. *Viewing any negotiation with your partner as a win-lose endeavour:* In a relationship with a life-partner, there is no such thing as a winner and loser. I often tell my client couples that no one in human history has ever won a fight or argument with a partner—if they do win a battle of some sort, all they 'win' is a hurt and resentful spouse, and that's a loss. All of your negotiations with your partner must come to win-win solutions.

8. *Forgetting that your partner is an independent, sovereign being who is sharing time and space with you, but nevertheless remains an individual:* This is big and the corollary is also true. Both you and your partner remain individuals first and partners second regardless of the perspective you take on it – physically, emotionally, intellectually, spiritually, and legally – you remain two individuals tied together by the choice to be with each other. To forget that is to lessen yourself and your partner in your mind's eye and you will likely fail to recognize the true nature of the gift you offer each other by remaining together.

Toxic Behaviours

These are the things people actually do that prove to be toxic in relationships. They are most often manifestations of the toxic attitudes and beliefs identified above. If you or your current partner exhibit any of these, then I strongly advise you both to do the work needed to eradicate them. If you are single and see any of these in a prospective partner, that should be a yellow or red flag, and in either case you would be wise to put a hold on any further development of the relationship until the problem is taken care of.

1. *Criticism:* Criticism, as opposed to invited constructive feedback, is a form of verbal assault. Expressing your own feelings about something your partner did or does is one thing, but asserting that he or she is somehow

defective or contemptible because of it is another.

2. *Trying to get your partner to change:* This one spells trouble in the attic. As a fundamental rule, if you cannot accept your partner exactly how he or she is, then get out. That doesn't mean you have to love everything about the person and doesn't mean you can't negotiate desired behavioural changes, but unless you can accept your partner fully, as is, you will be tempted to try to force unilateral changes, which is an assault on his or her integrity.

3. *Refusing to negotiate reasonable, requested behavioural change:* Let's face it, no two people are entirely compatible. There will always be friction points, and negotiating behavioural changes is a healthy part of a good relationship. If you are not willing to bend for reasonable requests, then you ought not to be there. If you are confused about an apparent contradiction between this point and #2, here's a differentiator. It is one thing to ask your partner to stop smoking in the house or car (a healthy behavioural request); it is another to ask him to be more ambitious (a character change request).

4. *Unbalanced sharing of business duties:* This means not pulling one's fair share of the myriad things it takes to keep a joint household running. If you add up the number of hours you each put into your careers (up to a 45 hour max), commuting time, and work in and around the house on shared duties, the numbers should be roughly equal. If not, it's like running a business partnership together with one person doing more of the work than the other…it will never work.

5. *Unbalanced sharing of the business profits:* What do I mean by this? It can be as simple as getting more recreation time at the expense of your partner, or having

one's personal finances profit more from your collective efforts. Example: both partners paying off a debt incurred by only one of them with no agreed means of compensating the assisting partner.

6. *Acting out of self-interest without considering your partner's reasonable needs and desires:* Taking care of your own needs and desires first is a best practice for you and your partner / family. Doing so at the expense of your loved ones can be selfish. Making certain you get out and play your beloved golf game is one thing; insisting you do that every Saturday while leaving your partner to take care of the household business is another.

7. *Invading privacy:* This includes stalking, eavesdropping on phone calls, checking pockets, hacking into or otherwise reading email, checking a partner's cell phone to see whom he or she has been in touch with. This is insecure and fundamentally disrespectful behaviour. Cut it out. If you can't, there may be a serious problem that is not being addressed, either with you, your partner, or the relationship itself. Do seek professional help before it is too late.

Emotional Clutter

Emotional clutter refers to the minor issues that arise in any relationship that have not been entirely resolved. Unlike unfinished business (see below), emotional clutter isn't as damaging but it can detract from the enjoyment of the relationship. Metaphorically, it's like letting your home become cluttered by the busyness of your lives. Not putting things away and not picking up after yourselves can leave a home feeling messy in no time.

The good news here is that emotional clutter is usually amenable to a quick pick-up. Like spending an hour or so picking up the house, you can usually put things back into place without much trouble. Having a good sit-down talk from time to time or a regular 'business meeting' will do this for you. Also, daily check-ins before bedtime is a great way for couples to air out their thoughts and feelings and take care of issues before they become a problem. It's like picking up the house a little before you go to bed – you always awaken to a fresh start.

Unfinished Business

Unfinished business is equivalent to having trash lying around the house – it clutters and stinks up the place and attracts vermin. For our purposes, unfinished business is any significant to serious issue that either of you have from your past that remains unresolved.

The issue may be something the two of you have conflicted on that continues to trouble you (garbage in the house). It might also be an issue from a previous relationship that is leaking into your present one (baggage by the front door). It might even be an issue from your past that continues to affect the way you're able to join someone in a relationship (a cracked house foundation). In any case, unfinished business can seriously affect a relationship.

If there is unfinished business between the two of you, it is critical that you tend to it as soon as feasible. Though you may be able to do this on your own, a short course of couple's counselling can help.

If the unfinished business is from past relationships, remaining single until you've done a thorough house cleaning is important; however, we are often not aware we have unfinished business until we are put to the test by a new relationship. Take heart, you can fix this problem if you take full, personal responsibility for it and seek help. Whatever you do, do not expect your partner to fix it, cater to it, or otherwise compensate for it. It's your problem, not his or hers...fix it.

Most troubling are issues from the distant past. Whether from childhood abandonment or abuses, or from bad experiences in relationships, the issues that can stem from those are often enough to drive any relationship onto the rocks without special care. My advice: take full responsibility for the problem and get help. Your partner didn't cause the problem and he or she cannot fix it.

Chapter 7

The One Year Agreement: Making the Virtual a Reality

"Let us never negotiate out of fear, but let us never fear to negotiate." ~ John F. Kennedy

How to Begin

In this chapter we explore what needs to be done to turn the concept of a One Year Marriage into a real, viable foundation for a healthy, enduring union. I will assume that you have read the previous chapters and have come this far because you're interested in the OYM as an option for yourself, as a mischievous imp to bottle up, or as an exercise in intellectual curiosity. In any case, reading with an open but discerning mind is always a good practice.

If the notion of creating a contract to define your relationship sounds unromantic to you, perhaps it is in the way you are looking at it. Planning for the future is a normal part of everyday life and a necessary task in any relationship that hopes to endure. Done poorly or not at all, it can weave a web of expectation and emotional dependency that detracts from the sense of security, self-esteem, and happiness of both parties. Done well, it can create a conscious and secure haven for the joyous side of the relationship – the love and passion you share. Accordingly, negotiating and contracting a OYM can be viewed as an act of love and a commitment to your individual and collective well-being.

As I've suggested a number of times in this book…

"There is only one good reason to be in a relationship with someone – because you truly want to."

One of the primary functions of a OYM is to ensure that this is and remains the case. Is placing one's heart on the line for unfettered love not a romantic act of faith and love?

Broaching the Matter

Discussing the possibilities of a OYM with a prospective partner is not as difficult as it might sound. In fact, I believe it can be easy and fun. Let's face it, both men and women love to talk about relationships and by the time most couples have moved into the stage of serious dating, they've talked about it for hours. If not, they're definitely outside the norm.

Although it's not exactly first date material, think about it… can you think of a more interesting, rich, and potentially contentious conversation topic to have with someone you might be interested in? Think of the possibilities – has he or she heard about the OYM? What does he or she think about it and why? Why is it a great idea or why does it suck? Just from talking about it with someone for an hour, I can guarantee you'll learn more about that person's attitudes and beliefs about relationships than if you'd known them for six months or more. You might also gain priceless impressions about what this person's expectations might be should the two of you hook up and get serious.

Though it may not be first date material (the mention of marriage of any sort will freak most people out), it could make for a great conversation starter at your local hangout or an appropriate social gathering. Could it help you screen out people you might not want to partner with? Definitely!

All that being said, it's likely that you and your prospective mate have talked about it. If not, it's time to broach the matter. The easiest way to do that is to be up front and relaxed. To simply ask your partner what he or she thinks about it (i.e., not specifically as an option for the two of you just yet) and to express your own thoughts and feelings about it is a great start. If marriage has been discussed before, or if you're already engaged, revisiting that is a great segue into it. Even if you are already in a traditional marriage, you can bring it up for fruitful discussion, which I will cover later. The key is to keep it light and fun.

The bottom line is this: two people who are living together or even thinking about it should be able to discuss anything relevant to your lives or the marriage. If you can't, then you have a problem that should be attended to sooner rather than later.

Even if the two of you have made no decision about living together or marriage, think about what you could learn about each other from having this discussion and doing the work of putting together a simulation One Year Agreement.

"If you cannot negotiate a mutually satisfying one-year agreement, chances are you'll not be able to negotiate the reality of a marriage or any long-term relationship."

So let's assume you have talked about a OYM and have decided to create a One Year Agreement, either to use or for the sake of the exercise and what you can learn – how do you start? Welcome to the fine art of negotiations.

Discussions & Negotiations

"Any business arrangement that is not profitable to the other person will in the end prove unprofitable for you."
– B.C. Forbes

The fine and gentle art of negotiation has nothing to do with the aggressive mayhem often portrayed about the blood sports of politics and business. It's not hard to see that many politicians and corporate execs appear never to have learned the truth in the above quote by Forbes, or have forgotten it. It is critical that we never forget this in our personal relationships because when it comes to those it's either win-win or nothing at all.

Perhaps it is best to think about this step of the process as the two of you co-creating an alignment that will provide a psychological nest for your love to flourish in. If you approach it with the same open mindedness and playfulness as you might when planning a great vacation together, you could actually have a lot of fun at it. In fact, one of my life mantras is…

If you're not having fun, you're not doing it right.

So keep it light, fun, and aim to come up with something that you can both embrace fully and enthusiastically.

So what do you talk about? You can start by thinking about all the things we normally have to do to keep the busyness of your lives flowing smoothly. There are your careers to look at and how many hours you each put into that per week, including commuting time. There is the work to keep the household in order (shopping, cooking, cleaning, etc.). Then there are the expenses to keep it all afloat.

Your individual roles and responsibilities should be discussed in reasonable detail. Don't just assume that the housework will get done or that your partner will pick up after him- or her-self. No detail is too small to consider. Articulating each other's needs and preferences now and formalizing agreements on them is one of the best investments you can make in your bond.

An important part of any relationship is the art of negotiation. Compromise is inevitable but how your partner negotiates or refuses to negotiate a one-year agreement can say a lot about his or her motives, philosophy, and ability to deal with you fairly.

Things to Consider

Sovereignty Protection

If the two of you are starting out fresh and without much social-financial obligation, then you'll find this fairly straightforward. It's simply a matter of creating an accord that recognizes and preserves all the good things about being single and autonomous, while supporting and nurturing your collective life.

Things to look at here might include agreements to make no claim on each other's resources brought into the union, to make no claim on resources individually acquired while in the union unless otherwise agreed upon, the maintenance of separate bank accounts, how bills are to be paid, etc. Another important consideration is to absolve each other of any and all debts accrued by the other before and while in the relationship. I've counselled a lot of angry, anxious people who, at the time of their divorce, discovered that his or her partner had considerable debts they hadn't known about (often from gambling or bad business decisions) and end up limping away on the hook for half of it. The essence is keeping your individual finances separate and creating a workable system for meeting your collective obligations (e.g., a joint account).

You might also want to discuss expectations regarding each other's social lives. How do you feel about her playing hockey three nights a week? How about his weekend 100 km bike rides? You might expect your partner to stop seeing that old flame he or she hangs out with once in a while. You might expect your partner to stop spending time with an ex-brother-in-law. The social expectations that can arise when we enter relationships can be quite significant and many go unspoken until the first argument about them erupts.

Though you can't anticipate all possible points of contention, it's a good idea to cover as many as reasonably possible, thus leaving less room for assumptions. As long as you agree to respect each other's *Social Sovereignty* and clarify what that means to the two of you, and then tackle as many hot spots as are obvious, you should have a solid foundation to handle issues as they arise in the future.

Pre-existing Obligations

Things can be a little more complicated when one or both of you have incoming financial or social responsibilities. Significant debt loads, a declared bankruptcy, or anything else that might affect you or your partner's ability to participate with equal time, energy, and finances to the relationship should be discussed with great care. It's critical to the success of the OYM that you come up with an agreement on how pre-existing debts will be allowed to affect your collective interests and what safeguards will be put into place to ensure that.

Similarly, if one or both of you have pre-existing social responsibilities that may impact the relationship, then they need to be discussed. An example might be children from another marriage. What role is the new partner to have in the lives of those children – auntie- or uncle-like, a parent figure? What are the hopes and expectations of each other in this area? What about significant social obligations at work? Some careers involve a considerable amount of hob-knobbing. Is the other partner expected to be part of that? Some require extensive travel while others extensive periods of absence, as with a military deployment. How will you negotiate those?

Mutual Investments

Eventually the two of you will likely want to make some form of mutual investment. Perhaps it will be something as small as a home entertainment system, or something larger like a home. Whatever their size or nature, it is important to agree on how you will divide mutually acquired resources should you allow the union to dissolve. Stating a set of principles and the actions to be followed to honour them should be sufficient, though big ticket items ought to be dealt with very specifically; the greater the investment, the greater the due diligence to be practiced.

Relationship Tip: Any major decision made within a OYM is best done only after asking a simple question: 'what if the marriage dissolves at the next anniversary?'

Unequal Resources

What if one partner has considerably greater financial resources than the other? How do you share things equitably? The short answer is in whatever way you consciously choose and feel is fair. As long as you do so with it clearly in mind that the union may dissolve in 12 months and you set up an exit strategy you can both happily live with, it doesn't matter much what goes on in between.

For example, if one partner can afford expensive vacations four times a year because she is a highly paid professional, then it is fine if she pays for them, as long as the terms of the exit strategy would balance things out for her should the union dissolve. Perhaps her partner would agree to some form of compensation, identified ahead of time and which can be paid at the time of severance. Perhaps it will not be an issue for her and the joy of spending the vacation time together may be enough compensation. Providing the partner with fewer resources does not expect to continue to live as though the wealthier ex-partner will maintain the higher standard of living, as we too often see with traditional divorces, there should be no problems.

Another option for this couple would be to take separate

vacations once or twice a year, or take vacations that are within the budget of their collective finances (i.e., that he can afford to pay for half of).

> **A *quick* note of caution:** *To gain full benefit from a OYM it is important to ensure that nothing compels either of you to remain together other than your love and your desire to share your lives. This can be corrupted when one partner has considerably greater material resources than the other and shares them in a way that the less affluent partner comes to enjoy a lifestyle not otherwise possible.*
>
> *Under those conditions, the less affluent partner's choice to remain in the relationship may be unduly influenced by the potential loss of lifestyle. At worse, the situation can lead to a subtle, perhaps unconscious power differential between the two, with the wealthier partner gaining the greater control. If there are significant differences in wealth between the two of you, be very careful of this!*

Another area where unequal resources can create problems is with major purchases or repairs. Ideally the two of you have been good at minding your personal financial affairs and are relatively debt-free and living comfortably beneath your means by a good 10-20% or more. When major repairs or expenses come along, you should both be able to manage them on your own.

For example, suppose the transmission goes in your car; ideally, you should be living well enough below your means to be able to pay for this, but what if you can't? Let's say your partner has $85,000.00 sitting around in various bank accounts and you have $14.73. One option would be to walk, bike, or take transit until you can afford to get the car fixed. Another would be to take out a bank loan to get it fixed now. Still another might be for your partner to pay for it with some identified means of rebalancing the books. She might even pay for the repair as an early birthday gift or a "just because I love you" gift (FYI – that's a gift only a guy would love). As long as such large, non-reciprocal transfers don't become a habit, there is no harm done. Should they become too frequent, however, it might become one of those toxic expectations addressed earlier in the book.

Not that the two of you can't make major purchases together. After all, when you're on your fifth agreement you might want to consider buying a house together. Just make certain the terms and conditions you set with each other in the agreement are fair and just for you both should the union dissolve next time it comes up for renewal.

If this all seems too cold and business-like – that's the idea.

Mind your own business and the collective business of doing life together will run smoother and happier.

I want to end this section with a brief case discussion to illustrate the importance of minding one's own business. I once counselled a man who, while he was married, had inherited a home after the death of a relative. In the jurisdiction in which they resided, that money was wholly his, and his wife could never have made a claim against it come divorce. As it was, the couple decided to buy a house outright with it. A few years later, the marriage broke down and the man was compelled to shell out half the appraised value of the home to his ex-wife – you've got to love community property laws. This is the point at which he sought counselling. Had he been in a OYM or at least used the relationship tip above, he might have opted to invest the money, minus enough to pay for the down payment, and bought the house collectively with his wife.

I've seen countless examples where people have made major financial, career, and personal decisions based on the presumption of marital permanence only to regret it later.

Would it cause you to think differently about the above example if it turned out the inheriting party had been the wife? Always treat the business side of your relationship as a win-win business, but a business nevertheless.

If you wouldn't agree to something in a commercial business partnership, you owe it to yourself and your life-partner not to agree to it within your relationship.

Accountability

The greatest made plans of mice and men are rendered to waste on a daily basis. Two of the most common reasons for this are a lack of action and its conjoined twin – lack of accountability. Accountability may sound like a form of overseeing and judgment but it's not. Creating accountability is really just arranging a way to track progress toward a desired destination, an alarm system to warn you when you're off course, and a set of procedures to help get you back on track. It's like a navigation aid on a boat. If you set the auto-helm for Hawaii and went below for a nap, you would be grateful if the system warned you of a malfunction that resulted in sailing north instead. That would enable you to make a needed course correction, unless of course you decided you preferred to sail arctic waters.

Accountability for our purposes simply means having a process wherein you and your beloved track how things are going and communicate about it. In its most assertive form, accountability may involve consequences, but they are always agreed on, light-hearted when possible, and never shaming.

Why is accountability needed? Most of us have numerous demands on our time and energy every day, many of which can feel important, even urgent. When pitted against the gentle call of attending to one's marriage, these daily demands can seem more compelling unless we take special care to prevent that. This is the principle reason why many people never quite seem to realize their long-range desires. You want to learn another language or how to play a musical instrument but never seem to have the time to do that. You want to write that book someday but someday never comes. It's a very old story that many an elder can share. Accountability then, is just a way to support your best intentions, to help you direct your focus and energies where you really want and need them to be.

Creating accountability is not complicated and you'll likely find that it happens naturally with the OYM. For one, you can expect to be more aware of the conditions of your union and how best to honour each other by virtue of the discussions you've had. You can also expect both of you to remain aware of the letter and spirit of your agreement because of the ever-approaching anniversary: the day of reckoning or celebration, of dissolution or renewal is no more than 365 days away and counting.

The best way to support each other in all this is to have daily check-ins to see how the two of you are doing personally and to clear up any problems from the day. It's also important to have weekly to monthly 'business meetings' wherein you discuss the financial / business side of the relationship. These check-ins and meetings can be fun and meaningful for the two of you, and it's a great time to discuss how each of you feels about all areas of the relationship. If you think meeting formally is unnecessary, imagine how soon a company would go out of business if they decided to forego the meetings of the board of directors and of management. Business is business and you're marriage, whether for one year or by traditional vow, is a business.

You can expect slippage in attentiveness and breaches of the agreement, but if caught quickly enough, they can be corrected without much work or damage. Sometimes this proves not to be the case, however and that is where consequences play a role.

Consequences to a breach can be very important to keeping the two of you on track and to demonstrate your ongoing willingness to really work on the relationship as you've agreed. Thinking of consequences as a way to help the both of you keep the relationship on the front burner will help you see them as supportive rather than punitive.

The strategy of consequences needs to be timely, relevant, reasonable, and non-shaming. It must be timely in the sense of offering immediate support – don't leave things up to year-end to settle because it will be too late then – fine tune things as you go. Leaving it to the end can also lead to growing resentment that can cause one or both of you to let the agreement lapse without renewal. One approach is to have those weekly check-ins and monthly 'business meetings'.

When consequences are honoured they must be timely as well. Let's say your partner has been neglecting the relationship by working too much and has agreed to reduce his work from 65 to 45 hours per week. If he has failed to do that by a certain date, then (assuming job loss is not an issue for the moment) a good consequence might be that he must reduce his work to 40 hours the very next week to help him make the shift.

Consequences need to be relevant to the breach. If your partner has a drug problem but has agreed to reduce his or her marijuana use from three times a week to once monthly within two months and she doesn't, a good consequence might be that she attends addictions counselling. It would not make sense to have her pay for your share of the rent as a consequence unless she believed that doing so would be a powerful and effective motivator to quit.

*Relationship Tip: Getting into a relationship with someone
with an addiction is risky and is usually a bad choice. You're
wise to assume that someone with an active addiction is
incapable of participating in a healthy relationship – period!*

Remember, consequences need to be reasonable and non-shaming. In fact, the whole process could be managed in a light tone and prove pleasant. Reasonable is relative of course, but the size of the consequence should roughly match the severity of the breach. This is something that should be discussed and agreed on. For example, if the above partner has engaged addictions counselling but after three more months he or she still blazes up excessively, the next consequence might be attending a residential treatment program within 30 days.

Keep in mind it's not about overseeing and punishment; it's about holding both of you accountable to an agreement that was forged in love and respect, and it deserves to be treated as sacred. Accountability is support to help us muster the best from ourselves.

Troubles at the Table

Okay, so what happens if you can't seem to get on the same page? What if repeated attempts to come up with a consensual, win-win agreement have come to naught?

One reason may be that one or both of you are resistant to the concept and process and are consciously or unconsciously sabotaging it. If you suspect that is the case, then go back over chapter six and discuss it together to identify and deal with your points of resistance. If resistance does not seem to be the problem, then there may be a deeper issue at hand that needs to be addressed before you proceed. Perhaps a course of counselling or couples counselling could be helpful. Please beware that counsellors can be quite conservative and may (unethically) push their own agendas. You can check ahead to determine whether your prospective counsellor is OYM-affirming.

Freeloaders

What do you do with a freeloader? Unfortunately the world is full of these sometimes quite charming individuals, and in hard economic times none of us are below their radar.

I suspect you will not have to worry very much about the most egregious of the freeloaders; the gold-, silver-, and bronze-diggers who are looking for a meal ticket. The prospect of a OYM is likely enough to scare them away since they are guaranteed to get nothing of yours when the union dissolves. However, if you have good and reasonably secure financial resources or live an enviable lifestyle, you could fall prey to someone who just wants to upgrade his or her lifestyle. This sort is always looking for a bigger, better deal so they're not that hard to figure out eventually.

The most troubling sort of freeloader is one you may not become aware of until well into your first, second, or even third OYM contract. This is the sort of partner who combines the qualities of being lazy and manipulative in a way that results in you doing or paying more than your fair share, despite your agreement. This is the sort of person who might minimize his or her breaches of the agreement and turn things around so that you end up feeling like a heel for being such a stickler. You may even be accused of not loving him or her enough or thinking more about the rules or money than about 'love.' Some of them are very good at what they do.

The best defence is to stand firm on your values and your understanding of the OYM agreement. Treat this sort of behaviour like you would if encountered in a formal business partner; hold them accountable, hold them firm, and be prepared to walk at the end of the year. It may be harder on average for women to do that than men, but if you've done your work in putting together the contract and retaining your sovereignty and social supports, it won't be nearly as hard as sticking with the lout or loutess.

Hardliners

Like freeloaders, these individuals might not show themselves until the first or second agreement is being discussed. The essential mantra of this sort is, "This is what I want and if that's not good enough for you then I'm out of here." They may put it a little or a lot more nicely than that, but the bottom line is the same.

The best way to respond to this is to sit back and look at what they are asking for. If it's more to do with them wanting some change for themselves and it either has little impact on you or they are taking responsibility for that impact, then perhaps you're dealing with a needed life change for that person. An example of this might be wanting to quit a job to go back to school. As long as your partner is willing to maintain financial responsibility for him- or herself, what is wrong with a little lifestyle change?

On the other hand, if what your partner wants are concessions from you with little to nothing in return, that should be a deal-breaker. In fact, any time the relationship swings out of balance so that you are not getting as much as you seem to be giving, that should be a warning sign that something is amiss and that it won't take too long before toxic entitlement begins to grind away at the foundations of the relationship. If you are both unwilling to work equally hard at correcting the problem, permitting the union to lapse and parting on reasonably good terms with self and resources intact is always an option.

Drawing up an Agreement

Once the two of you have had fun planning out your first year together under your initial agreement, it's time to put it all down on paper. A good starting point would be to use a viable prenuptial agreement as a model and go from there. There are many free templates available for download from the Net, but it is best if you use one that meets the legal requirements of your state or province.

There are two parts of a OYM agreement that need to be completed. One is a legal document that clearly articulates:

- The term of the agreement with a clear statement of complete dissolution on the anniversary date;

- The nature of your relationship (e.g., living as matrimonial or cohabitating partners) and its temporal limitation;

- The waiving of claims against each other's pre-contractual properties, financial resources, etc.;

- The waiving of claims against each other's personal financial and material gains during the period of the contract, including any form of spousal support;

- An absolution of each other from all debts the other has solely incurred during the period of the contract;

- Any previously agreed upon debts to each other (e.g., a $10,000.00 loan for a new car; compensation for taking time from work or career to raise children, etc.);

- Any legally enforceable issues you've agreed to (e.g., division of shared property, child custody and access, etc.).

The other part of a OYM agreement is the behavioural contract, which is enforceable only by the two of you. It is the articulation of how the two of you have agreed to honour each other's needs and wishes over the year of the contract. Anything within reason that is considered important to either of you can be placed in the agreement. From not smoking in the house to cleaning the toilet bowl once a week, nothing is too trivial if it is important enough to either of you. I think you'll find, however, that a lot of the small things come together of their own accord if the big ones and the fundamentals are addressed.

It can be as simple as a typed document stating, "I, Jamie X, agree to honour my beloved, Jesse Y, by striving to do my utmost in doing the following during the coming year... then you can fill it up with all the things you've agreed to do and not do. Your partner would fill in his or her as well, of course.

It may seem like a lot of trivial formality but you'll find it's easier than it looks and it does set a strong benchmark to adhere to. It may be nice to promise something to someone, but words are exceedingly inexpensive and in the realm of the virtual; once spoken they are vulnerable to being forgotten, distorted, or outright denied. It's much better to clearly state something in writing and to then sign and date it. In psychology, this is sometimes called a behavioural contract, and if done properly and reviewed regularly, it can be an effective means to guiding behaviour.

Of course, the only thing that matters at the end of the day, or in this case at the end of the OYM agreement, is whether the two of you lived up to your promises. That fact will help determine the agreement for the following year, or whether an agreement will be made at all.

Legalities

Ah, yes, our favourite realm – the foggy, obscure realities

of the legal system. Let's face it, the legal systems in North America, particularly in regard to family law, are broken and will not likely get fixed any time soon. My professional experiences have taught me that fact. It's rather disconcerting when you hear lawyers and police officers alike assert that we don't have a justice system; rather, we have a legal system that either rules for you or against you, and justice or fairness sometimes hold little weight.

Obtaining Legal Advice

Despite all that, I do think that it's wise to obtain at least a brief legal consult on how to ensure your OYM agreement is recognized and enforceable in your state or province. There may also be laws in your jurisdiction that impact what you can and cannot make a part of your agreement. I don't think it necessary for you to have a lawyer draft up the agreement, but if you have the coin and are so inclined, by all means do so. If you do have a OYM agreement and your lawyer has assured you it meets all legal requirement, and if you're willing to share it with others, please feel free to send a blank copy of it by mail c/o Moontide Books, or by email (oneyearmarriage@gmail.com). I will do my best to make it available on my website (gsrenfrey.com) as a free download.

If you seek legal advice, don't expect a warm reception or optimistic approval. As mentioned elsewhere in the book, the legal system in North America is adversarial and lawyers tend to have a win-lose mentality despite their best intentions. In the business word, lawyers are deal breakers, not deal makers, and are usually kept out of the business negotiations until it's time to draw up the papers. It's not their fault; it's the way the system is set up. In fact, your lawyer will not even be able to represent the two of you together.

Do share whatever legal advice you receive with your betrothed, and use it to inform your co-created agreement.

Don't get bogged down with the madness of the legal system, but, as with a self-written will, do make certain your agreement meets your state or provincial standards to be legally enforceable. Use legal advice to make certain the two of you are honoured in the way you want and to make your agreement with each other legally bullet-proof, but use your love and negotiations with each other to make it a win-win.

Recognition by the Courts

It's hard to predict how the courts of your state or province will interpret the nature of a OYM but there are a couple of possible predictors.

One clue is the status of prenuptials in your state or province. Do the courts always honour them? Do they ever overturn them and for what reasons? Are there things that cannot be included in a prenuptial (e.g., in Ontario, the marital home is mandatory community property, regardless of who owned it prior to the marriage)? Another is the status of common-law marriage where you live. Do the courts recognize it? At what point does a couple become recognized as having a common-law relationship? What are the legal and financial implications of this?

The courts overturn prenuptials sometimes, as when one party is destitute and the other is not. With the OYM this seems unlikely unless your partner had a very serious and rapid turnaround in finances. That could happen (hey, maybe she had everything in Enron...), so it is best to check with state or provincial laws to ensure that your assets are protected from the misfortunes and bad choices of your partner. Sound cold? It's not – you can help him or her out as much as your heart desires. Being forced to do that against your will, however, is financial rape, which can have major emotional consequences.

One possible way to add a layer of protection for you and

your partner is to agree to penalties and compensation should one partner successfully challenge the OYM agreement in court, or should it otherwise be overturned. Perhaps a separate compensation agreement in the event that a court does overturn part or all of your OYM agreement and one of you is hit with a financial assault. Perhaps the compensation agreement would allow you to make a dollar-for-dollar claim against such amounts as may be awarded to the other party. Do seek legal advice about the viability of such an agreement in the courts.

A OYM may not be recognized as a marriage in your state or province, or may be recognized only as common-law marriage, if even that is recognized. The only way this will affect you that I can see is in regard to tax breaks for married couples, social security / social insurance, employee health and extended health insurance benefits, etc. Best check into these if they are important to you.

Children and the OYM Agreement

When it comes to child custody and access, what the courts decide is in a child's best interest will nearly always trump an agreement. Of all the aspects of a OYM agreement, the ones that may be most vulnerable to being overturned by a court of law are stipulations about how the custody and access of shared children will be managed.

As I address in chapter five, battles over child custody and access can be heated and damaging to all parties involved. Even if you're both model parents with solid, respectable careers, icons of mental and physical health, with close, loving relationships with your children, and can each provide them with an ideal home environment, it would not stop either of you from taking each other to task in a vicious, win-lose court battle over 'who gets the kids.' It's a sad state of affairs, yes; more evidence that the system is broken. As discussed in detail in chapter five, however, if you do justice by each other across your OYM agreements you'll minimize the chances of this sort of madness from ever happening.

Do include this in your agreement if you do share children. Decide, while you are in love and have each other's and your children's best interests in mind, how you would like to ensure their continued care. Remember that, all things being equal, children are best served by having equal access to both parents.

One Year Marriage Conversions

As mentioned in early chapters, the OYM model is a flexible way of governing the relationship with your life partner. It is possible to shift into and out of a OYM as your needs and desires change. Below is a brief sketch of some of the possibilities, though you and your partner might well end up living something entirely custom designed. It's the new millennium – there are no rules.

An Upgrade from Living Together

If the two of you are currently living together or are thinking about it, why not try on a OYM for size? The benefits of doing it are legion. Not only will you discuss critical issues for your relationship and come to a common understanding on them (or not), but you will learn a lot about each other and how you work together. You have nothing to lose and everything to gain by using a OYM agreement as the basis for living together.

Converting from a Traditional Marriage

If the two of you are already in a traditional marriage but want to try the OYM – great idea! The easiest way to do that is to negotiate and create an agreement and sign it on your anniversary as a way of reaffirming your commitment with each other. Although your traditional marriage will not dissolve on your next anniversary, your 'virtual' OYM will.

Getting into the habit of honouring each other and your relationship in this manner is a great way to keep your relationship fresh and alive.

Although it doesn't have the possibility of a real marital dissolution as a motivator, you can still enjoy many of the benefits of a OYM. If you love it, you can always divorce and live by OYM contract alone. The philosophy and practice of the OYM is unconventional and most people seem to lean toward convention in major life decisions. Because of that, I suspect that traditionally married people living by one-year agreements will tend to outnumber those using any other permutation of the OYM.

Converting to a Traditional Marriage

One possibility you might consider is converting a OYM into a traditional one. This would make the process similar to the ancient Celtic tradition of the handfast, wherein a couple would make a vow of marriage for a year and a day, after which they either parted ways or vowed a more permanent union. So you see, the One Year Marriage is not so avant-garde after all, as I discovered after the first edition of this book – it's been around a very long time.

After one or more successful OYM contracts, you might feel an overwhelming need to become conventional, or perhaps you decide it's a little too avant-garde for raising children. Whatever the reason, nothing prevents you from getting married in the old-fashioned way at some point. If you do that, you can always live by the OYM process of renegotiating and contracting for another year, as discussed above, thereby continuing to enjoy many of the benefits.

Letting the OYM Lapse

Finally, for one reason or another, the two of you might decide to let your OYM agreement expire, yet continue to live together. This is essentially converting a OYM into a common-law union. You might do this because the two of you 'get it now,' and it seems like too much fuss to renew the contract. Do keep in mind, the conventional wisdom that successful marriages are a lot of work; that work is precisely the kind of fuss the OYM demands – remaining aware of your and your partner's desires, doing your best by each other to meet those desires, making conscious choices within the marriage, and holding each other lovingly accountable for your agreements. That is the work of a good marriage. That is the work of enduring love.

Chapter 8

Doing The One Year Marriage – Better, Deeper, Broader

> "Your time is limited, so don't waste it living someone else's life. Don't be trapped by dogma – which is living with the results of other people's thinking. Don't let the noise of others' opinions drown out your own inner voice. And most important, have the courage to follow your heart and intuition." ~ *Steve Jobs.*

Doing Relationships Better

The One Year Marriage is designed to help couples form happy, satisfying, and enduring relationships. However, as an approach to life, it can take you well beyond that. There are deeper and broader benefits to embracing impermanence and retaining personal sovereignty as a way of doing life. Most of these you will discover on your own, as you should, but in this chapter I have sketched out a few that I have personally realized. First, however, I want to share a few final suggestions for doing marriage, be it traditional or unconventional.

Dee Chinimini is a parenting and relationship coach and consultant to Moontide Books. She has co-authored this section to provide perspective through a woman's eyes.

One Year Marriage / Relationship Tips

- If you're wondering with whom to spend your life, just think to your last day on earth and ask if this is the person you'd want to be with. If it is, then you know you've made a good choice; if not, then go in search of the one you'd want to be with and don't settle until you've found her or him ~ DC

- The best way to have a happy marriage is to prepare for it. Rather than focusing on finding the right person, direct your attention to 'becoming' the right person— who do you need to be? When you think of your ideal partner in your ideal lifestyle, whom do you need to become to fit into that picture and to draw that partner to you? What do you need to do to create that lifestyle to share? ~ GSR

- Don't ever ask your partner for 'permission.' Do inform him or her of your intentions, out of respect and courtesy, and do be open to altering your plans based on your partner's reaction, but you never need permission to follow your heart's desire. ~ DC

- Live as though the only thing binding the two of you is your love, and then act to make it so. Eliminate anything that could hold the two of you together against your better judgment, or desire. Cultivate a marriage of two independent lovers joining in voluntary interdependence, and you can build the sort of relationship people only dream of. ~ GSR

- Most women have a strong nurturing instinct. In marriage, we can fall prey to placing the needs of our mates and children ahead of our own, as though that is our responsibility, as though we believe "if they're happy, we'll be happy," but it's never true. When we do that, it's not long before we've compromised our own well-being and happiness. Instead, perhaps we should use our instinctive skills to teach each member of our family how to co-create peace and harmony. ~ DC

- Take time for yourself – daily. One of the core benefits of setting aside time for self-care comes from the very act of taking time for you. Doing so means you are saying "no," if only temporarily, to all the other demands regardless of how compelling they seem. That act alone affirms your health and happiness as high priorities. The busier we become, the greater the importance of doing this. Stepping off the mental treadmill helps ensure we keep things in proper perspective, and tend to our needs. Remember, a healthy, happy you is the best gift you can give your beloved (and your children). ~ GSR

- Never surrender your financial independence. Always be able to support yourself. Financial surrendering is an entrapment; it gives the other person power over you – power and control you never want anyone to have. Always know you can support yourself. ~ DC

- Borrowing from the wisdom of Morrie Schwartz,[33] it behoves us all to ask a simple question of ourselves with faithful regularity: if my marriage were to end tomorrow, would I be ready? If the answer is 'no', then ask 'what must I do to be ready?' By keeping ourselves accountable in this way, we can help ensure we remain effective, sovereign participants in the adventure of love and marriage. ~ GSR

- Don't be afraid to walk away; the world will not stop and you will not die. Although it may feel that way for a time I promise you that after three months (if not sooner) things will look different, and you will feel different ~ DC

- Run the 'busyness' of your lives like a business. Be excellent business partners with clear expectations, lines of communication, fiscal responsibility, and a fair and painless exit strategy. Always aim for win-win outcomes in the business side of the relationship and make it a habit of re-evaluating, renegotiating, and either dissolving

---

33   Mitch Albom (1997). Tuesdays with Morrie. Random House, New York.

or renewing the contract every year on the anniversary. ~ GSR

- If it comes time to parting ways, move on with respect – don't devalue what you had with each other. They say we should leave a person in the same state we met them in or better – don't leave your partner worse off. Live your life with compassion and respect. Leave a relationship on good terms, with compassion and respect. ~ DC

Deeper Benefits

The OYM and Happiness

I believe the benefits of practicing the philosophy and method of the OYM go well beyond a desirable and enduring love; I believe it's a powerful means to creating a happy, fulfilling life. Much of its power to do so lies in embracing impermanence, something counselled in the text of Buddhism, Christianity, and every other great spiritual tradition I'm familiar with. Much of its power also lies with the practice of being aware of your needs and life path, and taking full responsibility for those.

How we do our most important relationship in life largely reflects how we go about our lives in general, but the opposite is also true – conduct your life with awareness, responsibility for self, and with acceptance of impermanence, and that will be reflected in the way you choose to do your relationships. What might this look like?

Put simply, you'll be inclined to be aware of your needs and desires, take full responsibility in creating a desired and fulfilling life for yourself, and deeply enjoy it by not clinging to the illusion of permanence. Once you've accomplished that, you'll not likely compromise it for anyone, but when you find a kindred spirit, one who has personal sovereignty and who has also created a desired life, the two of you will have the greatest gifts to offer in a loving relationship. You will likely choose only a partner who can bring the same gift, his or her ideal life, to be shared freely without expectations.

An important ingredient to happiness in the quest for love is to be complete within our own skin. I believe the only true way to find a love that is deeply fulfilling is to evolve ourselves to sufficient completeness that we lose the 'need' for another. When we have enough love and respect for ourselves to be able to stand alone, only then can we enjoy a bond that is based on true appreciation for self and partner without expectations.

As a way of conducting ourselves and creating a desired life, a sense of inner completeness and personal competence is a core requirement for true happiness. It is the foundation of personal freedom, self-determination, knowing what you deeply desire, and learning to get your needs met through your own actions. It's about being aligned with a purpose and engaged in your life path. That adds up to freedom, satisfaction, and meaningful living. For me, that's the ultimate benchmark for wealth.

The OYM Promotes Personal Growth

It has been said that few people evolve in their consciousness during the core of their adult years—between their 20s and early 50s.[34] I don't believe this is necessarily the case, but I do believe most people impede their personal growth during this life stage by becoming overly busy.

Growth before our mid- to late-teens is a given because of innate physical changes that take place, and the natural challenges of needing to get out and find a way through life on one's own. When we hit our stride by our mid 20s however, most people tend to become overly busy with external concerns; whether it's career, a mate, raising a

---

34. Ken Wilber, *Kosmic* Consciousness. Sounds True (2003).

family, or just plain having fun, most people appear to become distracted from the central life-task of personal growth and evolution.

Although a career and relationship are both potential venues to growth and satisfaction, becoming lost in either is detrimental in the long run. By retaining a clear focus on your personal life path, by making it your central priority, you can find the balance of self-actualization, relationship bliss, and career / life-work evolution.

The OYM helps prevent us from becoming lost in relationships. As a template for doing life, it encourages recognition of the impermanence of things, and the reality that life is indeed a solitary adventure. With that comes a persistent directing of one's attention to the personal meaning of all things around us, and that is the means to self-actualization, to finding deeper meaning and satisfaction.

Accepting that life is essentially a solitary journey is a daunting notion for most and a terrifying one for many. However, by recognizing and accepting that each of us enters this world alone and leaves it in the same way, we open our minds and hearts to compassion. Accepting this truth helps us to see how alone and vulnerable we all are; to appreciate how precious it is when we offer to share our unique experiences of life; and opens the door to deeply intimate connections, perhaps even to grace – a connection to the divine, however you conceive it.

Broader Benefits

The One Year Career

Using the OYM model as a way of doing life has a natural extension to career. As mentioned in the previous section, losing one's self in a career is unhealthy and, in the larger scheme of things, counterproductive. At the end of your days, it will not matter to you how successful you were in your career or how much money you made. What will matter is how deeply you experienced life, how much you evolved as a person, and how well you loved and were loved.

A career can be a deeply satisfying endeavour that provides for the material needs in life and acts as a venue for personal growth, providing one does not become lost in it. Lost is lost—period! How can we prevent that from happening while embracing our life-work as an important venture? On cue – enter the One Year Career.

The true impermanence of jobs has become a glaring reality in the last few decades. Few if any of us have any real income security. Confidence that one's material needs will be met (food, shelter, and warmth) is important as it allows us to focus on the higher things in life, such as personal growth. However, relying on an employer or any single source of income ensnares us in a state of dependency. To assume relative permanence in an income source is to lull one's self into a false state of security and complacency.

As discussed in chapter two, people tend to take their jobs for granted when they presume relative permanence. With that comes lower job performance and satisfaction. When job security is assumed, people also tend to make poor financial decisions and overextend themselves with unwise spending. The matter is complicated by the fact that few of us are not caught in the addiction of materialism to some degree. I believe the current debt crisis is at least in part due to a presumption of job or income security. Is the use of constructive insecurity in the form of presuming job impermanence a solution? I believe so, at least partially.

Take a moment to imagine that, whatever your job, you only have a one-year contract with your employer and you are not guaranteed that it will be renewed. If you are self-employed, you can imagine that something might happen in a year to compromise your professional credentials or current customer base. Would you do anything different from what you are doing now? Would you be more aware of your job performance and the marketability of your skill sets or products? Would you spend differently? Would you, for example, go into debt to buy that shiny new car when the five-year-old model you own looks and runs great?

I suspect that if people assumed and remained aware that their current jobs could realistically end in one year, and they weathered it in a healthy way (proactively) they would likely:

- Be more aware of their job performance;

- Find more satisfaction in their jobs;

- Keep their jobs in healthy perspective and not sacrifice health, relationship, or happiness for them;

- Be more aware of their marketable skill sets and be proactive in remaining marketable;

- Be more aware of their debt load and mindful of their spending;

- Take greater charge of their financial well-being and ultimately feel greater financial freedom.

Don't get me wrong; I'm not suggesting people should pessimistically look at their future prospects as though disaster were around the corner. I am asserting that if we recognize the real possibility that our current job may not exist for us in one year, that we will be stimulated to engage in a more mindful and self-realizing life of personal responsibility. I have no doubt that many would slip into denial or the fog of addictions in response to anticipated job loss, as I've witnessed in friends and clients for decades, but that issue is beyond where I intend to go here.

Final Words

Writing the One Year Marriage was an act of joy and service. Marital unrest and unhappiness have become commonplace and yet we continue to give it our best shot, sometimes time and time again. In working with couples over the past few decades I'd come to believe that we, as people, as a culture, are failing in our most intimate relationships. Then it dawned on me that perhaps it was how we were trying to go about it, that the model we were using to guide us was the core of the problem. What we needed was a fundamental change in our way of doing marriage.

The One Year Marriage represents an attempt to provide a different way of looking at and doing the institution of matrimony. Though there is nothing technically new about any aspect of what I've proposed, approaching this most important of relationships as a relatively short-term alliance with no presumption of continuance is a fundamental change. As such, I anticipate it will be resisted by most and vehemently criticized by many. However, if the OYM encourages readers to think about their relationships more consciously, if it enhances their awareness of how they choose to embrace another into their lives, then I feel I'll have made a positive contribution to the quality of their marriages and lives. If it stimulates interest in finding alternative approaches to helping people partner more effectively, all the better.

How you choose to respond to what I've written is all that matters and is itself an act of sovereignty. Whatever your choice, power to you – I wish you all the luck and joy in the world. Please feel free to share your experiences and comments directed to oneyearmarriage@gmail.com, and with your kind permission I will share them with other readers by way of the One Year Marriage blog on my website at 'gsrenfrey.com'.

With that I leave you with one of my favourite quotes:

"Security is mostly a superstition. It does not exist in nature. Life is either a daring adventure or nothing...."
~ Helen Keller

Appendix

Explorations

**"In wisdom gathered over time I have found that every
experience is a form of exploration."** ~ *Ansel Adams*

This section of the book contains five explorations to
help you clarify and affirm what you want from a partner
and a relationship, and what type of marital union would
serve you best. It also contains an exercise to help you
identify your relationship deal-makers and deal-breakers, and
one for assessing the state of a current relationship as it
relates to the ideals of the One Year Marriage.

As with any form of self-exploration, you'll get out of it
what you put in to it. If you complete the explorations with
curiosity and an open mind, you'll likely get the most from
your efforts.

Exploration 1 – Your Ideal Partner

This exploration will help you explore the thoughts,
feelings, and images you have about your ideal partner and
the life you want to share. Although you'll start out creating
a simple wish list of partner attributes, you're asked to go
beyond this to create a more holistic impression of your
desired mate, and how he or she fits into your desired
lifestyle. This 'hologram' of an ideal partner and way of
being together is a good way to ensure the partner you are
seeking is one you'll be happy with.

Some of us are very conscious of the type of partner and
relationship we want, while others are open-minded and
accepting of what may come. In either case, knowing your

likes and dislikes, your deal-makers and deal-breakers, is an essential place to start in the process of co-creating a deeply satisfying union. Keep in mind that what we think we want is not always best for us and that sometimes life has a way of offering surprises that prove to be better options.

This exploration is done in five steps and it is best if you follow the sequence as presented.

Step One: Create a wish list for how you want your partner to be. What are his or her most important attributes? What are the most important qualities he or she must embody? What are things you would not want him or her to do or be like? Are there any deal-makers? These are things so important to you that without them you may not be happy (e.g., good communicator). Are there any deal-breakers? These are things you know would be fatal to your happiness (e.g., a drug or gambling addiction). Write these out and ponder them for a few moments. Do you have a rich idea of what he or she is like? Do you get a good sense of how he or she would feel to be with?

Step Two: Now imagine that you are blind—how would you want your partner to be? How would you like him or her to behave, talk, and feel like to be around? Spend time thinking about this because it may be the most important question you will ever ask yourself about your desired partner. Choosing a partner as though you were blind is a good way to ensure you choose wisely and not simply for superficial reasons. If any new traits surface here, add them to your list of deal-makers.

Now imagine that you have sustained a serious injury or illness and will be convalescing for more than a year. How would you want your partner to handle this and what character traits would he or she need to posses?

What if you became wheelchair-bound? Now imagine it is your partner who has become ill or injured. What qualities would he or she need to posses to make you want to stay in the game? Make a note of these as well.

What about financial downturns? Imagine you have lost your financial means and have encountered more difficulty than you'd expected getting back on your feet. What traits would you want your partner to posses? What if the roles were reversed? Record these.

It is important to consider how undesirable circumstances might affect your choice of partners as life does send challenges our way and some can be severe. If you want an enduring love, it's best to consider how your relationship would stand up to unforeseen misfortune, and what qualities your partner needs to posses to ensure this. If you haven't already done so, make a note of these traits and consider adding these to your deal-makers. You might also challenge yourself here – do you posses them?

Step Three: Now imagine you can see, and are of sound mind, body, and finance. Take time to envision your ideal lifestyle while keeping your partner in the background for now. Imagine the look and feel of the life you would create for yourself were you to become financially independent. Now take it down a few notches to envisage a reasonable lifestyle to aim for given your current resources and trends. Try not to be too lavish here and don't focus just on material wealth or objects – focus on your lifestyle, on the things you would do from day to day, on how you feel when you awaken in the morning and then go about your day. Identify any qualities of this way of life that you believe are crucial to your happiness. These will be the core characteristics of your ideal shared existence.

Step Four: Starting from where you are in life now, imagine you're about to move forward into your ideal lifestyle. Starting with the core partner characteristics you identified in steps one and two, does your ideal partner fit well into that journey and existence with you? Are there other qualities he or she should posses to make it a good fit? Take a few moments to imagine this person working toward that way of life with you or otherwise supporting you in your quest, and then living your individual dreams together. Make notes on who this person is and what he or she is like.

Step Five: Now it is time to consolidate your findings. If you haven't already done so, make certain the results of steps two and four are integrated into the wish list from step one. Have your partner ideals shifted at all? One of the best ways to organize a list like this is to categorize items into desirable and undesirable qualities, and to use the most critical of these to create short lists of deal-makers and deal-breakers. It is important to be especially careful with your list of deal-breakers, as these are traits that, if you detect them in a potential mate, should dictate an immediate termination of the relationship – there should be no concessions on these.

When choosing a partner, it is expected that you will make some compromises, that you will not get everything on your desirables list, and you may get a few items of your undesirables (which, BTW, is fine if you can assume those will never change and you can completely, honestly accept that); however, deal-breakers are exactly that – "No Deal, Honey"! Once identified, it is best to consider it a sacred duty to ensure it is respected, or if it is revised, that it is done because you recognize the item should not have been on the list in the first place.

To complete this exploration, you can write out a brief

description of your partner in prose, or simply organize your likes, dislikes, deal-makers, and deal-breakers into a chart to review and reflect upon.

Exploration 2 – Your Ideal Union

Though it may appear to overlap with Exploration 1, here you will examine your ideals about love and relationships more than your ideal mate and lifestyle. This will help you determine the core elements of a good marriage for you. These are qualities that you deem essential to a happy union. Once known, you'll be able to explore the deeper motivations behind them.

Step One: Similar to the first exploration, write out your wish list for what your ideal relationship will look and feel like. What are the core, most important characteristics of this union for you?

Now take time to imagine your ideal lifestyle as you did in the first exploration. It's likely easy to imagine your ideal partner and you living your ideal lifestyle within your ideal relationship so go ahead and do that. Did anything new reveal itself?

Now take a few minutes to imagine that hard times have struck. The inevitable failures and disappointments that life brings our way have come to affect the two of you. How would you hope the two of you would weather the storm? What attributes would allow your relationship to do well in hard times?

When you're done, create a list of the qualities you just identified. If you can, group them into logical themes.

Step Two: Take this list of essential relationship characteristics and see if you can distil them down or otherwise identify the four or five most important. Now it is time to explore each of these to a deeper level.

Begin with the first point and ask yourself what is important about it. A good way to do that is to repeatedly complete the sentence, "when I have that, it will get me . . ."

For example, if you identified **security** as an important feature, then it might be important for you to ensure it is a part of your relationships. A deeper exploration of this could reveal several ways of obtaining it, however. This would consist of asking yourself what the valued feature would get you, and then asking what that would get you in return, and so on. Eventually, you will come to a core desire; one that is so fundamental it cannot be broken down further. For example: a deeper exploration of **security** might look like this...

Security will give me **freedom from fear of abandonment.**

Then...

Freedom from fear of abandonment will give me **happiness** and **peace of mind.**

Then...

Happiness will give me ... Hmm? **Happiness** (a core human desire – no need to go deeper)

And...

Peace of mind will give me **comfort.**

Then...

Comfort will give me... Hmm? More **comfort** and perhaps **peace of mind,** both of which are common core desires. This sort of circular loop is usually another sign of reaching a core desire.

In the above simple example, the deeper desires behind the value placed on security in a relationship were a desire to be free from the fear and abandonment. It would have been possible to explore what it is about abandonment that is so frightening. This was not done for simplicity's sake here, but I do recommend that you trace your connections to their roots and explore them fully. When you do, you may find that the things you desire in a relationship are only ends to deeper means and that you have other options, often more reliable and healthy to obtain.

In the above example, by developing an internally referenced sense of security, the individual would lose much of the 'need' to depend on someone or a relationship to provide feelings of safety. With that would come wider relationship options and greater confidence and freedom within a partnership.

Exploration 3 – Your Ideal Relationship: Which Model Fits Best?

In this exploration, you will use the results of Explorations 1 and 2 to compare how core qualities of your ideal partner and shared lifestyle, and your ideals about love and relationships match up with the traditional and One Year Marriage models. The purpose is not to convince you that one model is better than another, but to help you examine your options. Since it assumes a working knowledge of the One Year Marriage model, this exploration is best attempted only after reading chapters one through five.

The exploration can be done in many ways, but one suggestion is to create three columns on a sheet of paper or e-document and label them 'Trait/Feature', 'Traditional', and 'OYM'. In the first column, list the desirable traits, deal-makers, deal-breakers, lifestyle features, and relationship essentials you identified in Explorations 1 and 2.

Now, for each in turn, imagine how that feature or characteristic might be played out in a contemporary marriage. Asking several questions might help in this – how well does a contemporary marriage support or encourage this? How would you respond within a contemporary marriage if this feature began to fade or fail? When examining your deal-breakers, how would you respond within a contemporary marriage to address this and how effective might that be? After you have contemplated this enough to get a good vision or feel for it, rate it from −3 (very poor) to +3 (very good) in how well a traditional marriage supports and encourages that desired item.

Now do the same for the OYM. It may take a stretch to do this as the concept of the OYM may be very new and still uncomfortable for you, but I encourage you to take a courageous stab at it.

Once completed, you can either take in a global view of how the two models compare and/or add up the columns. How did they fair? You may find that one model supports some of your core values and desired characteristics better, while the other better supports others. If you did yourself justice and completed the exploration fairly and earnestly, you should be in a good position to evaluate your options for a marital union. Any choice that is informed and made with one's eyes open is better that one based on assumption.

Exploration 4 – Sizing Up Your Prospective Mate: Guidelines For Choosing a Partner

It may seem presumptuous to include a section here on choosing a partner – after all, what could someone else possibly know about your needs and desires. However, I believe some basic principles and guidelines are helpful in seeing through the miasma of thoughts and emotions that arise at the start of a new relationship, and making choices that will bring you the love you deeply desire. Most of the guidelines presented identify traits and habits that are negative or positive indicators of a good partner, while some address your own feelings.

You may have heard or read of many of these tips because few of them are unique to this book and most reflect common wisdom. Recognition, however, is vastly different from understanding something at a useful level, so if you simply scan and skip the ones you think you know, you may miss something important to your future happiness.

My challenge to you is that you actually think about each of these with a beginner's mind – even if you are so familiar with an idea that you can't bear to contemplate it further, try asking yourself, "why **is** this important?" and "how does that apply to me?" Better yet, try explaining aloud to an imaginary friend why it is important and how it would help you choose a good partner to set up shop with. That is the true measure of understanding.

As you work through this section, try thinking about how you stand on each of the guidelines presented. You might place some of the positive indicators on your wish list and identify others as deal-makers. Similarly, you may place some negative indicators on your 'exercise caution' list and identify others as deal-breakers. Once you decide where you stand on each, you'll have a rough set of personal guidelines to follow. These are not written in stone and could change as you do, but it's advisable to commit to honouring yourself by respecting your guidelines.

I've organized this section into three subsections – Gathering Information, Positive Indicators, and Negative Indicators.

Gathering Information

When it comes to gathering information about a new or potential partner, nothing beats the old axiom, "*It isn't what they say, but what they do that matters.*" Actions do speak louder than words and it's not just because there are people out there who would intentionally deceive you. Under the best of circumstances, what people say about themselves is notoriously unreliable and often inaccurate. Why? Because words are a function of virtual reality, the representation of self and the world that sits between our ears. The problem with that is simply this – there is always an imperfect relationship between our virtual realities and physical reality.

Our perceptions of others and ourselves are prone to distortion by attitudes, beliefs, desires, emotions, and dozens of other factors we need not go into here. At the end of the day, it means that most people are not capable of describing what they are like accurately enough for you to base your choices on. Add to that the usual desire to make a good impression on a prospective new partner and you have a perfect formula for very misleading self-descriptions.

It also means that you will not likely be capable of assessing a prospective partner's character without a few well-thought-out and reliable benchmarks to guide you. There is hope, however, as embodied in the simple axiom…

What people say about themselves is usually a less reliable gauge of what they're really like than seeing them in action. Remember – 'It isn't what they say, but what they do that matters.'

Psychologists have a dirty little secret – despite all our standardized, scientifically generated tests and ways to analyze and predict behaviour, the simple truth is – the best predictor of behaviour is past behaviour. True, people do change over time and some radically so, but in the absence of any substantial, discernable process that could generate such change, the most reliable predictor of a person's behaviour in a given situation, is his or her past behaviour in a similar situation.

What does this mean for you? Exploring his or her track

record of relationships and carefully observing what your prospective partner does under certain conditions can speak volumes about what he or she is like to partner with. A word of advice for any such exploration:

> *What you see is what you get. If you cannot accept someone just as he or she is, then get out quickly – this must be your relationship Prime Directive. Trying to change someone to meet your preferences is a loser's strategy that can only lead to pain for both of you.*

With that in mind, here are some possible explorations to consider:

1. Imagine you are blind. How does it feel to be with this person? A great piece of advice given by Clarissa Pinkolas-Estes some years ago was "Choose someone as though you were blind."[35] We are so often swayed by appearances that they can cloud our better judgment. Research has shown that people often wrongly perceive good-looking people as possessing more positive attributes than the not so endowed.

   Of course we all want a gorgeous animal to hang with, but appearance actually contributes little to the quality of a relationship. Besides, appearances do change and if you're hoping to be with someone for a long time, you'd best examine how they 'feel' to you as though you were blind, because that is something that can endure and even sweeten with the ravages of time.

2. Explore your partner's relationship track record. I am not referring simply to dating partners, but significant relationships that lasted six months or more. Stay out of the bedrooms of the past (very, important) but do try to find out how long your partner's last three or

---

35. Clarissa-Pinkola Estés (1996). How To Love A Woman: Myths and Stories about Intimacy and The Erotic Lives of Women. Sounds True, Boulder, CO.

four relationships endured, why and how they ended, and whether he or she is still on good terms with the exes.

Talking to ex-partners directly is good; though beware of grudges and ex-bashing. Common friends can be a good source as well. What to look for here is a pattern of reasonable stable relationships that end on a positive note with no hard feelings. Without that, your relationship with this person will likely end badly.

3.   Explore your partner's financial track record. The size of his or her bankroll is not important here – it's more important how he or she manages finances. How someone handles money says a lot about how they handle life in general and will predict what you will be dealing with in running the business of your lives together.

Things to look for include consistency of income, debt load, spending habits, saving habits. Another valuable piece of information here is whether or not your partner has lived alone and managed to run his or her personal finances independently: some people may appear fiscally viable, but in fact they have always relied on someone else – if not parents then partners – to keep them afloat. The ability to support one's self without external assistance is an important indicator of mature, personal responsibility.

4.   Related to the above, has your prospective love lived alone and managed his or her personal life well? How did he or she fare? Is there evidence that this person has created a personal life that he or she loves without someone else woven into it? The bottom line – do they have a great life to share with you, or are they expecting to hitch a ride on your life, or start over from scratch?

5.   Go for a drive. How someone drives is a great personality projective. Even if your prospective partner is trying to make a good impression on you, he or she will have a tendency to drive unconsciously (i.e., as per usual), unaware of what they are revealing in the process.

I heard of a company who used a post-interview drive to lunch as a final test of candidates. Though many candidates looked great on paper and did well in their interviews, once behind the wheel, some drove aggressively or discourteously, some proved to be too hesitant and could not assert themselves in traffic, while others demonstrated the desired traits of assertiveness and courtesy.

There are other less critical indicators that you can glean from someone's driving. These include such things as taking up two parking spaces, doing laps in a parking lot just to get a space close to your destination, excessive speed, tailgating, excessive slow driving, poor judgment – the possibilities are limited only by your powers of observation.

6.   You also learn things from the cars people choose and how they treat them. It's always important to ask why they pick the cars they do and not make assumptions, but a few broad generalizations can exemplify how exploring this can be fun and informative. Is the car bare-bones minimalist but practical – many aspects of your life together may prove to be that way. What sort of image is he or she trying to project and why? Does the guy driving a big pickup use it for work, is he perhaps compensating for low self-esteem or a sense of low status, or is it because of something completely different? Did the woman in the expensive car buy it because of the way it feels, rides, and handles, or is she

trying to impress others, to exert some sort of status? Is driving an ugly or unpopular car due to being independent (self-referenced) and really loving something about it, or is it due to bad taste?

Using a car as a moving trash container suggests he or she will likely keep a messy house as well. Excessive concern about its appearance can reveal an overvaluation of appearances. There are countless possibilities but remember... explore, don't assume.

7.   Workout together. How we conduct ourselves in the shared space of a gym can say a lot about the kind of person we are. I've been amused countless times at the gym observing someone turn a tidy exercise station into a chaos of weight plates lying around the floor or left on the bars for others to put away. Have you ever been distracted from your workout by someone repeatedly dropping a bar full of plates or otherwise making unnecessary noise? You'll have your own things to look for, but some to consider include: does s/he clean up after themselves; share the space well with others; exhibit focus; or wander around and workout haphazardly?

8.   Play house for a weekend. This is a little tricky because it implies that the two of you have become close enough to be spending a weekend together. Nevertheless, spending time with people in a living situation can give you an idea about how well they keep house (or fail to). Does she pick up after herself in the bathroom? Does he share with the housework? Things like that are important over the long haul.

9.   Fashion anyone? People differ widely in their preferred fashions. Although there are no absolutes in fashion and no right or wrong ways to be fashion-conscious, conflicts can arise when two people differ too widely in

their fashion sense. Noting whether your prospective partner is a slave to fashion, dresses to please him- or her-self regardless of trends, or is a self-professed trendsetter can save hassles in the future.

If there is a conflict in this realm, remember the Prime Directive – can you accept this person in your life exactly as he or she is? If not, you have yourself a deal-breaker – trying to upgrade the wardrobe of someone you perceive as less fashion-conscious is a toxic practice (unless that person asks you to) and it might be an indictor of a deeper issue of non-compatibility.

Those are a few of many ways to gather information about your partner. Now what do you do with all that information in hand?

Positive Indicators

These are signs that your prospective partner may be good relationship material. None are definitive, but they are significant and cumulative. Take the opposite of these signs as negative indicators.

- *Communication:* Can s/he communicate thoughts and feelings well and understand yours? Communication – the ability **and** willingness to clearly express what we honestly think and feel, and to understand what our partners think and feel – is the lifeblood of a relationship. It takes skill and it often takes more courage than facing a live machine gun, but without it, no relationship can flourish.

- *Laughter:* Does he or she have a good sense of humour? Your partner does not need to be a comedian, but he or she does need to recognize the comedic side of life and self. The ability to get a joke, take a joke, laugh at life, and laugh at one's self are essential to a balanced and happy life.

- *Respect:* He or she shows genuine respect for you, self, and others. Respect is not just deference because of some anticipated consequence (e.g., with one's boss or a traffic cop) – it is holding one's self and others in reasonably high regard and acting accordingly. If he or she demonstrates respect, especially when there is no clear payoff or this (e.g., respect toward a street person), it is the sign of a socially healthy person.

- *Compassion:* Buddhists hold compassion as one of the highest virtues. In selecting a life partner, a compassionate heart is a sign that your prospective mate isn't lost in self-interest and is capable of empathy. Such people tend to be understanding and giving in relationships, and are more likely to be able to see outside of their own belly buttons when things go awry. The subtle, everyday signs of compassion (e.g., braking for squirrels) are more telling and reliable than writing large checks to charities.

- *Life-Work Balance:* Does your prospective partner balance life and work? It is far too common for people to fall prey to the 'work to get ahead' trap, and if you're in a relationship with such a person, guess what – you'll get trapped as well. A career does take more time and commitment than a job, especially when you're trying to establish yourself, but even at the peak of career sacrifice, retaining a needed degree of balance should be possible.

  If your prospective partner is in a demanding field, are there periods of intense work, separated by periods of greater life focus, or are they constant? If your partner is caught up in a time-intensive commitment (e.g., is in medical or graduate school), is there a commitment to reducing workload at the earliest opportunity. If not, you may be partnering with someone's career, not with them.

Negative Indicators

These are signs that your prospective partner may be poor relationship material. None are definitive, but they are significant and cumulative. Take the opposite of these signs as possible positive indicators.

- *Addictions:* Any sort of active addiction should be a deal-breaker. If you're in a relationship with someone with an addiction, be it to gambling, drugs, or alcohol, then **you** have an addiction problem – he or she may be the practicing addict, but make no mistake, **you** will pay a heavy price. The minimal price you'll pay is being number two in your partner's relationship priorities. Advice – get out before you get burnt.

- *Intimidation:* Do you ever feel intimidated by your partner's emotions or behaviour? Unless you have an issue yourself with not tolerating other people's emotions well, this is usually a very bad sign. Your partner should be able to feel and express any of the range of human emotions and you ought to be able to remain present and engaged without feeling intimidated or stifled. If not, then either your partner is not ready for a relationship or you're not. Take a break and try again when the problem is resolved.

- *Competitiveness:* Our culture nurtures and rewards competition, but excessive competitiveness is the harbinger of a legion of toxic personality quirks. Whether it is due to latent anger, low self-esteem, or antisocial personality traits (BTW – they used to call those psychopathic traits), if your prospective partner doesn't have his or her competitiveness well-bridled (e.g., drives aggressively; can't lose a game without getting upset), he or she will be incapable of sustaining a healthy relationship with you.

Remember, a critical part of a OYM plan is having a win-

win exit strategy. Should the two of you decide to end things (not renew your agreement), you'll want to walk away on good terms. However, if your partner is excessively competitive, you'll likely face an opponent who wants to hurt you and win all the cookies. If you have a problem with being too competitive, do yourself and your future partner a huge favour and seek therapy before you enter a relationship.

- *Discourtesy:* If your partner exhibits discourteous behaviour toward others, it's another sign of trouble with relationships. How we treat strangers speaks volumes about our orientation to the world. Discourteous behaviour (as when driving) suggests the person sees the universe as an unfriendly place and may have a lack of respect and empathy for others. Do you really want to live with that sort of energy?

- *Self-Importance:* Does he presume excessive self-importance or take herself too seriously? Though each of us is at the centre of a unique universe and within that universe we are the most important person (or should be), a healthy ego will recognize that other people are the most important people in their unique universe as well. In that, no one is more important than anyone else in any general sense. Presuming self-importance is a sign of an immature personality or inflated self-opinion, both of which are deadly to healthy relationships. Avoid at all costs if you know what is good for you. Similarly, people who take themselves too seriously, who cannot laugh at themselves from time to time are usually vexatious to live with.

If you ever find yourself breaching a mate-selection guideline that you've decided to follow, you're well-advised to hold yourself accountable – explain to yourself or a friend, why you're making the compromise.

Exploration 5 – The Relationship Scale

Introduction

This questionnaire is designed to be a quick exploration of the health and happiness of a relationship. You can use it to explore past, current, or desired relationships, a comparison of which can be quite instructive in helping you identify their strengths and weaknesses.

The Relationship Scale is based on the OYM values and philosophy that are embodied in the following – two people in love, each sovereign and independent, happily sharing their lives with mutual respect, equitable interdependence, and nothing to bind them together other than their love and desire to be with each other. You don't, however, have to share that ideal to use or benefit from the scale.

The scale is broken down into 10 sections, each representing a key element of relationship health and satisfaction. The distinctions are somewhat arbitrary and may not include something you consider important, in which case simply add any additional elements you want.

To use the scale, simply rate each item in each section using a scale of –5 (extremely bad / not at all) to +5 (extremely good / completely) with the zero-point being neutral. When done, you can obtain the average score for each section (the total score ÷ number of items answered) and enter it on the provided graph, or one of your making, to yield a visual of the relationship as a whole. For any items that do not apply (e.g., regarding children, if you do not have and plan not to have any), then leave the item blank.

The Scales

Love and Emotional Intimacy

1. How happy are you with the love and emotional

intimacy of the relationship? [____]

2. How would you rate the way your partner expresses love toward you? [____]

3. How would you rate your feelings of love toward your partner? [____]

4. How would you rate the level of emotional connection between the two of you? [____]

Total = ____ (Add scores) **Average =** ____ (Total ÷ Items)

Physical Intimacy

5. How happy are you with the physical intimacy of the relationship? [____]

6. How do you rate the amount of cuddling and other non-sexual physical contact you share? [____]

7. How would you rate your satisfaction with the frequency the two of you have sex? [____]

8. How would you rate your satisfaction with your sexual exchanges? [____]

Total = ____ (Add scores) **Average =** ____ (Total ÷ Items)

Communication

9. How would you rate how well you feel understood by your partner? [____]

10. How would you rate how well the two of you are able to express yourselves freely and respectfully? [____]

11. How well are you each able to hear the other accurately when discussing things? [____]

12. How well are you able to talk about difficult problems and successfully resolve them? [____]

13. How well are the two of you willing and able to work through things when upset with each other? [____]

Total = ___ (Add scores) **Average = ** ___ (Total ÷ Items)

Quality Time

14. Overall how happy are you with the amount of quality time you spend with each other? [___]

15. Rate your satisfaction with the amount of undistracted time with your partner to do the things the two of you enjoy? [___]

16. How happy are you with the things you do together that generate a sense of shared enjoyment or adventure? [___]

17. How happy are you with the time you spend together with friends or your children, doing things as a family / group? [___]

Total = ___ (Add scores) **Average = ** ___ (Total ÷ Items)

Shared Values

18. How compatible are your basic values? [___]

19. How compatible are your views about relationships and how they are best done? [___]

20. How compatible are your parenting philosophies and styles? [___]

Total = ___ (Add scores) **Average = ** ___ (Total ÷ Items)

Business Partnership

21. How happy are you with the way the two of you do the 'business' side of the partnership? [___]

22. Considering both employment and household work, how happy are you with how you share the workload? [___]

23. How well do the two of you share the financial costs of your relationship? [___]

24. How well do the two of you agree on major financial issues? [____]

25. How well have the two of you been able to co-create an agreeable financial strategy? [____]

26. How compatible are your saving and spending habits? [____]

Total = ____ (Add scores) **Average** = ____ (Total ÷ Items)

Sovereignty

27. How strong and intact is your personal sense of identity (i.e., the sense of you as an individual outside of the relationship)? [____]

28. If your relationship ended tomorrow, how well would you guess you would be doing in six months? [____]

29. How well do your think your partner has done in retaining a strong sense of personal identity? [____]

30. How strong is your sense of independence? [____]

31. How strong is your partner's independence? [____]

32. How well do you respect each other's rights as individuals? [____]

33. How well do you respect each other's rights to personal privacy, time, and space? [____]

34. How well do you respect each other's rights to personal friendships? [____]

35. To what degree do you feel free of the need or desire to control your partner in any way? [____]

36. To what degree do you feel free of attempts by your partner to control you? [____]

Total = ____ (Add scores) **Average** = ____ (Total ÷ Items)

Personal Finances

37. How well have you 'minded your own business' – i.e., how well have you ensured that your personal finances and career have retained their viability outside of the collective interests of the partnership? [____]

38. How well has your partner minded his or her own business? [____]

39. To what degree have the two of you discussed and agreed-upon an equitable, win-win financial exit strategy from the partnership? [____]

Total = ____ (Add scores) **Average** = ____ (Total ÷ Items)

Security

40. How emotionally secure do you feel the relationship is? [____]

41. How secure do you feel in your ability to go it alone and support yourself in life? [____]

42. How secure do you feel in yourself in committing to a relationship based on a one-year term? [____]

Total = ____ (Add scores) **Average** = ____ (Total ÷ Items)

Scoring and Graphing

A quick way to graph your results is to calculate your average scores for each section and place an "X" for that score, above or below the corresponding category on the graph provided at the end of this section.

Do you notice anything interesting in your scores? For the most part, the first five categories are general and would apply to any healthy union regardless of the model followed. The next four categories relate more specifically to relationship characteristics needed to make a OYM work. How did the relationship you assessed fare? Could it have been readily transformed into a OYM?

```
+5                                                                      +5
+4                                                                      +4
+3                                                                      +3
+2                                                                      +2
+1                                                                      +1
 0-----EI-----PI-----C-----QT-----SV-----BP-----S-----PF-----S-----0
-1                                                                      -1
-2                                                                      -2
-3                                                                      -3
-4                                                                      -4
-5                                                                      -5
```

May you find someone very special, and cultivate
an enduring love. ~ G.S. Renfrey

About The Author

Dr. G. Stephen Renfrey is a clinical psychologist, life-coach, and author. He received his undergraduate degree in zoology and psychology at the University of Toronto and went on to work and study at the University of British Columbia. He completed his graduate training in clinical psychology and holistic health care at Western Michigan University, and was a staff and adjunctive faculty member at the Michigan State University Counseling Center before deciding to pursue a full-time private practice.

Dr Renfrey is a lifelong practitioner of yoga and meditation and has pursued lay-interests in sociobiology, cultural anthropology, and diverse other fields. Combined with his training in holistic health care and his more than 25 years of clinical experience, he brings a balance of scientific, metaphysical, and spiritual perspectives to his work.

Dr. Renfrey has authored numerous pieces for academic texts and journals, but in recent years he has turned his attention to publishing books for general readership. This is his third non-fiction, self-help book, and he has authored works of fiction. He continues his private psychological practice in Ontario, Canada and can be reached at oneyearmarriage@gmail.com or through his website – gsrenfrey.com.

About Dee Chinimini

Dee Chinimini is a parenting and relationship coach, and a frequent consultant to Moontide Books. She can be contacted via her website: heart2heartcoaching.ca.

www.ingramcontent.com/pod-product-compliance
Lightning Source LLC
Chambersburg PA
CBHW031621040426
42452CB00007B/611